A
Different
Conversation

Realizing your potential as a real estate agent

Mark Winter

Tellwell Talent
www.tellwell.ca

ISBN
978-0-2288-1412-2 (Paperback)
978-0-2288-1411-5 (eBook)

Table of Contents

Foreword ix

Introduction to Changing the Real Estate
Conversation xiii

Section 1 The Partnership Framework............................ 1

Learn the refreshingly new and unique way to work
together that this framework provides and understand
with ease the value this brings to your conversations.

1. Ladies and Gentlemen ... Introducing the
    Partnership Framework Pyramid 2
2. Twelve essential elements of partnership............. 4
3. Eight essential elements of thought-
    provocation 14
4. Six essential elements of being creative 18
5. Eight essential elements of inspiration 21
6. Four essential results of boosting potential..........27

    Summary of core principles and self-reflection... 35

**Section 2 The Elevator Ride to Successful
            Partnership Communication**..........................37

When we set ourselves and our clients up in "presentation
mode," we tend to impose limitations on the potential of
both the immediate conversation and the longer-term
working relationship. How can we better frame out our
working relationship and mutually fulfill its potential?

1. Connecting through the Elevator Ride, not the elevator pitch!.................................38
2. Understanding the eleven Core Competencies of the International Coach Federation..41
3. What are the four responsibilities of the coach, as defined by the ICF?.....................43
4. How real estate agents interpret what coaching means...45
5. Are you naturally curious?.............................52
6. Let's use the framework!................................54
7. Are you open to a paradigm shift?................58
8. What do you believe about preparation and change?..59

   Summary of core principles and self-reflection...61

Section 3 Our Role, Our Value, and How We Compete 64

Understanding the fullness of our role can be challenging, especially in the context of using similar sets of presentation tools to try to out-compete each other.

1. What is our role? 64
2. How do we choose to compete? 70
3. On what actual basis do you compete?...........72
4. Our perception of what our value is 75
5. Assumption of expectation 76
6. Why **prescribe** and **pronounce**? 79
7. Perspective itself...82
8. What happens when a client asks for my opinion? 84

   Summary of core principles and self-reflection...86

Section 4 Conversation and Presentation Perspectives

Section 4 Conversation and Presentation Perspectives 88

Real estate sales as a career has traditionally been very presentation-driven. Stop for a moment and consider: how can your clients benefit if you adjust your approach?

1. Harnessing the power of collaboration to level the playing field 88
2. Reflecting on typical coaching 92
3. The coexistence of conversation and presentation.. 102
4. That word: "closing"................................. 108
5. Scripts versus proficiencies..................... 109
6. They say buyers are liars?...................... 111
7. So, when *is* it a presentation? 113
8. Communication options 115

   Summary of core principles and self-reflection.. 119

Section 5 Mastering the Conversational Contract

Section 5 Mastering the Conversational Contract 121

What does it mean to actually *engage*? What effect can it have when we are able to work as a team in the journey from initial conversation of discovery all the way through to possession of a new home?

1. A conversational contract—what is that? 121
2. Uncovering the real topic for you and your client to focus on................................. 126
3. Guide your client to open up and explore the conversation by getting some balls up in the air! 127
4. Refining focal points for the conversation 129
5. The agenda—whose is it?.....................131
6. Four brilliant partnering questions to establish a high-value agenda 132

7. The check-in during a long conversation 134
8. Check-ins versus pronouncement 135
9. Identification of what the client hopes to
    walk away with from the conversation 139
10. Paraphrasing 141
11. Reflect back to your childhood! 143
12. Think about possibilities and the importance
    of the language we choose to use 144

    **Summary of core principles and self-
    reflection** 145

Section 6 Understanding some of the Structural Elements and your own norms 148

**How do we show up? How can we best equip
ourselves and establish a more effective start
with clients? What defines our success?**

1. What does professional presence mean? 148
2. Creating working guidelines with your clients .. 150
3. Working with congruence and vision 153
4. Reframing how we approach an interview 155
5. Redefining our interpretation of hard skills 160
6. What's in your tool belt and tool chest? 161
7. What does success breed? 166
8. Do you need to disarm the entitlement trap? .. 168

    **Summary of core principles and self-
    reflection** 169

Section 7 Circumstantial Confidence 172

**Our own personal confidence—and that of our clients—
is the foundation upon which we are able to make life
decisions. Understanding the enablers and disablers
of confidence can help us be at our most effective.**

1. Confidence with conversations that span the career bridge.................................. 174
2. Confidence with conversations for generating new clients......................... 177
3. Confidence in maintaining client relationships with those in your database......... 179
4. Confidence in a potential seller or buyer appointment........................... 182
5. Confidence in actual listing or selling transactions............................ 184
6. Confidence with after-sales care 185
7. Confidence around your peers.......................... 187
8. How can you employ mindfulness to help your confidence?................................ 189
9. Passion and positivity.................................191
10. Is vulnerability holding you back? 192

    Summary of core principles and self-reflection 193

Section 8 Conversations in Buyers', Sellers', and Transitioning Markets 195

How do changing market conditions affect the focus of our conversations?

1. Finding opportunity in a slow buyers' market . 196
2. Finding opportunity when transitioning toward a buyers' market.................................... 197
3. Finding opportunity in a balanced market..... 197
4. Finding opportunity when transitioning towards a sellers' market 197
5. Finding opportunity in a hot sellers' market 197
6. Fixation with price 205
7. What about the transitioning markets?.............207

Summary of core principles and self-reflection 208

Section 9 Skills development that will advance you ahead of the crowd 210

Essential skills that will enable you to outperform others on the playing field, and, most importantly, increase value for your clients.

1. Sensing versus thinking 210
2. **Asking** to **advising**—the transitional bridge 211
3. Positive acknowledgement and handling tougher questions 215
4. Delivery considerations 219
5. Silence and space: turning awkwardness into thought-provocation 220
6. Head to the source of your client's goals, not the solution! 222
7. Listening choices 225
8. Powerful questions 228
9. Powerful questions that involve visualization 235

Summary of core principles and self-reflection 238

Summary 241
Epilogue 243

Foreword

Have you ever wondered if there was a better way for real estate service providers and their clients to engage? Do today's consumers really want to be talked at, presented to, persuaded, and convinced?

What this book offers you is core professional coaching principles in a simple, easy-to-understand format that challenges and provides refreshing alternatives to these typical sales interactions and how your dialogues flow. It is a valuable resource to real estate conversations from a coaching perspective and delivers results for you as a real estate agent by building higher-value working relationships, by helping you to realize your potential for growing and sustaining a successful business, and by allowing you to enjoy your work even more than you already do. Can you make more money, have an easier life, and enjoy your career more by embracing the concept of coaching your clients? The potential of coaching is limitless.

Professional coaching is all about a conversation of discovery and finding out what a client wants to achieve, and then drawing out some of their own self-generated solutions and a plan to reach them. As you will discover in this book, coaching principles apply effortlessly to the realm of real estate conversations, and as precise competencies and frameworks are revealed you will be able to create a refined and refreshed vision for your future client interactions and for your real estate business. How exciting is that?

I have spent over thirty years of my life in the real estate industry and I am a Professional Certified Coach (as designated by the International Coach Federation—the ICF). I have had the privilege of working alongside some exceptional people—in real estate sales, management, and organizational coaching—and it is through these great experiences that I am able to bring together the core principles of coaching and show you how they can readily and effectively apply across a multitude of real estate service interactions with your clients.

I have facilitated the learning and adoption of this subject matter for multiple groups of agents and their valuable feedback has contributed to the vast value and depth of this material. I have been pleasantly surprised how immensely passionate I have become about coaching agents on how *they* can coach *their* clients, and inspired by their tremendous feedback. It has been the most successful and experienced agents I have coached who have articulated the most profound belief in the principles set out in these pages.

I believe there are three main reasons why the drop-out rate in our industry is so high: agents cannot find enough clients to serve, they run out of financial resources and patience, and they fundamentally misunderstand their role and how they compete for business.

To help you stay and grow in a successful career in the business, **this book will help you compete effectively** in the most important competitive area of all: the conversational realm with clients.

As an agent, are you frustrated at being unable to bring your clients to a decision as markets ebb and flow? Do you enjoy that feeling of having to justify why you should be the agent selected to work with by a client? Do you find it hard to truly differentiate yourself? Would you like to build deeper, more effective working relationships with your clients on a consistent basis?

You will discover herein the potent blend that I have created that brings everything together—my Partnership Framework and Elevator Ride are combined with the ICF Core Competencies and responsibilities of the coach to create a new and unique take on real estate conversations. I am confident that you will also discover some rich nuggets, those inspiring *a-ha* moments that happen when you suddenly realize that there is something refreshingly new and exciting to adopt as part of your competitive advantage.

At the beginning of each chapter, simple learning objectives are set out in point form. As each chapter ends, these are reiterated and combined with some thought-provoking questions to help you consider your operational, conversational, and behind-the-scenes business approach.

As a coach and an author, I am committed to making a positive difference for your business and in helping you reach your life goals. You'll learn to break new ground and bring more value to conversations with clients, from the perspectives of both yourself and your consumers.

Introduction to Changing the Real Estate Conversation

Time is racing by and uncertainty looms over the horizon. The way we work has become dated and anachronistic. Operating procedures set out by licensing authorities are becoming ever more stringent. Almost a quarter century ago, the Internet threatened to change the profession's very existence; yet today, face-to-face communication is still the bedrock for how the most effective dialogues take place.

What I absolutely love about coaching is that its possibilities are endless. It's modern and progressive conversation; it's authentic and spontaneous. You can pair 100 clients with coaches and you'll have 100 different conversations. Yet we all help our clients generate solutions as we dance freely in conversation under the guidance of known professional principles.

Coaching-based conversations offer exciting options for real estate interactions and will be a high-value, in-demand portion of real estate service in the future. They provide clarity of thought for your clients and heightened awareness of all the pieces of the puzzle involved in the decisions that they need to make.

This book is about having a *different* conversation to those that have been led by agents in the industry for years and aims to support you as a front-line agent in your real estate sales role by imparting awareness and perspective, but it will also help you **compete in a different way** for business and **work more effectively** with your clients. You will be able to take a fresh look at both your value to your clients and how you can sustain a business. **It will fundamentally question your urge to *present*** and you will learn a new framework that enables partnership, alignment, and more effective communication, so that your relationships with your clients become clearer, deeper, and more meaningful, offering a greater chance of a mutually successful outcome. This book will help you build some exciting new skills to offer; it is structured to help you better understand your role, and to both develop and refine your own operating system.

It is no secret that some view our industry with disdain, and its professionalism from both internal and external viewpoints has certainly been openly questioned in many markets in recent years. **Let me help you stay on the high-value end of the spectrum and embrace competencies that will fuel your business into the future.**

We do a pretty good job of shining a light on ourselves in this industry. Personal branding used to be scarce twenty-five years ago; today it has developed to such an extent that it is sometimes hard to simply ascertain which brokerage an agent is associated with. One goal of this book is to help us, as an industry, shine the light on our clients through deeper collaboration rather than operating in ways that seem to justify why we should be the ones selected to work with, trying to out-compete and out-market each other. It is time to look at how we can build value in a different way.

As a backdrop to this work, there are several points that need to be made by way of context. Firstly, it is important to start out by recognizing the excellent efforts that so many agents in our business are making to enrich their clients' lives and to help them attain their real estate objectives. There are lots of wonderful people in our business. Secondly, this book is not meant to suggest that the way some agents compete for business is wrong—not at all. In reality, there is rarely only one way to achieve something, and the concepts in this book aim to challenge norms and encourage new ways of approaching the business of guiding clients successfully. I am confident that by adopting this modern coaching framework, participating agents will not only stand out and increase their opportunities for more business, they will also forge longer-lasting relationships with even more of the consumers they interact with. This book will help you refine *how* you work and how you approach your career, to incrementally increase the value of your professional service.

So, whether you are a consistently high-producing agent or new to the business, are you up to the challenge of finding more natural ways to engage clients and add another component to your own value proposition? Do you want to move forward and develop a language with your clients that will help you engage with each other in greater depth and with more openness and collaboration? Or would you prefer to continue along the same conversational path trodden over decades that will inevitably become less and less effective, and eventually put you out of touch?

I would like to thank all the people who have inspired me to put this work together. I have met so many amazing people through the coaching programs at the University of British Columbia, through the International Coach Federation Vancouver Charter Chapter, and also many of the coaches I have met globally through ICF. The ICF is a global organization founded in Kentucky that provides codes of ethics and standards and certification for its members. Their vision is simple: "Coaching is an integral part of a thriving society and every ICF Member represents the highest quality of professional coaching." Their Mission: ICF exists to lead the global advancement of the coaching profession, with around 35,000 members in 77 countries at time of print.

Special recognition goes to British Columbia–based coaching professionals Donna Howes, Ceyda Gultan, Jayne Tellier, Heather Turnbull, Kathy Taberner, Michael Newland and Karen Flynn, as well as to Kevin Tomkins (based in Alberta). Their spirited support of my writing journey has been wonderful.

Most notably, to Lynn Hsu and Dan Scarrow for their openness and willingness to develop and integrate a coaching culture into Macdonald Real Estate Group; to Bill Dick for his review from the perspective of managing broker; to our other managing brokers for their endless support; to real estate professionals Glen Jessup and Carissa Siy for their positive encouragement and feedback; to Jonathan Li, who created most of the imagery and also inspired the cover design; to Rosey Hudson, for her support and guidance on integrating this book into the industry; to all the experts at Tellwell publishing, who have added their professional polish at each step of the way; and to the hundreds of agents who have actively participated in the coaching sessions and courses, and who have provided such profound and encouraging support for this cutting-edge approach.

The collective brilliance of all these wonderful people mentioned above has inspired me to be a leader of change for the real estate industry; so, from my heart, a great big thank you to each and every one of you.

Quick note: I use the terms "consumer" and "client" loosely and for ease of illustrative examples, as markets work differently in terms of definitions and agency. For simplicity and ease of learning, please interpret these words as being someone you are engaged in any kind of real estate conversation with.

These coaching principles and examples are designed for adherence to the professional responsibilities of real estate licensing authorities.

Section 1

The Partnership Framework

Learn the refreshingly new and unique way to work together that this framework provides and understand with ease the value this brings to your conversations.

Learning objectives are to understand:
- **What the Partnership Framework is**
- **What the five keys words mean in our context**
- **What actually happens when we partner, provoke thought, create, inspire, and boost potential**

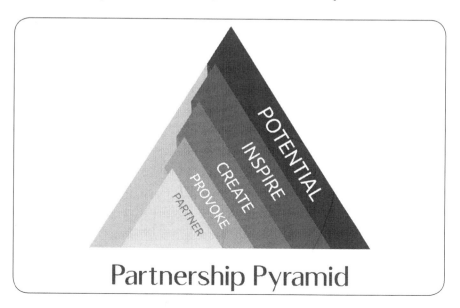

Partnership Pyramid

Ladies and Gentlemen ... Introducing the Partnership Framework Pyramid

One evening in June of 2017, I found myself sitting in my hotel room and looking out at the view of Victoria on beautiful Vancouver Island. It had been a great day engaged in coaching dialogues with a dozen professional real estate agents. I had this tremendous sense of curiosity as I allowed my mind to contemplate how to simplify the whole idea behind coaching for those involved in service. I wrote out the International Coach Federation's definition of coaching:

> Partnering with clients in a thought-provoking and creative process that inspires them to maximize their personal and professional potential.

As I carefully examined the words, it became very clear to me that five of them really stood out from the rest:

> **Partnering** with clients in a **thought-provoking** and **creative** process that **inspires** them to maximize their personal and professional **potential**.

The light bulb started flickering as I began to arrange them in the order of an inverse pyramid:

Potential
Inspire
Creative

Thought-provoke

Partner

Why? For me, the very basis of a successful conversation is its foundation: the partnering.

I then started to think about how to clearly define each of these five elements and then to frame them in a way that made sense. It seemed far too simple to say, "Go and form a working partnership with your clients." This is a bit like saying, "Just go and bake a cake." What are the ingredients? As time has passed by, I have slowly and carefully added and refined these elements.

In subsequent classes I found that this way of communicating coaching was starting to make real sense, and soon enough these five elements formed a key part of my group learning sessions.

As I look back, my intention was not to turn agents into coaches—there would not be sufficient time for that within the context of our individual workloads. My goals instead became raising awareness amongst my peers of the core competencies that professional coaches learn, sharing these principles in the simplest way possible to advance and accelerate learning, encouraging agents

to be more curious, and encouraging them to follow the pyramid structure.

So, let's jump into the pool and take a detailed look at each of these five elements, shall we?

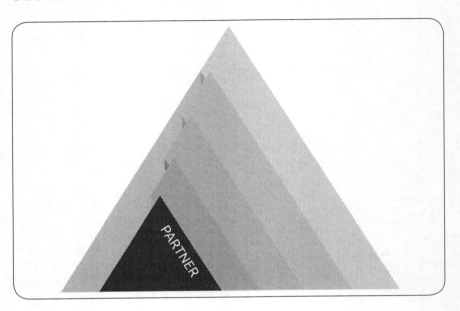

Twelve essential elements of partnership

So, what happens when we *partner*? Below are twelve essential elements of partnership that really stand out for me.

1. **We collaborate** – Conversations take place in the spirit of togetherness as we work toward a common goal.

2. **We engage both mind and heart** – When we are able to encourage a client's thoughts and emotions in combination, we take them to a place they might not find on their own. We also engage their souls as their passion is activated, and that

connection comes back positively to you as a partner.

3. **We ask powerful questions** – Simple language drives to the heart of the matter. Powerful questions that serve to engage mind and heart might be: "What did you think about that?" followed by "… and how did it make you feel?" Think for a moment about how our questions land—if you read these two questions out loud, one right after the other with the same rate of speech and tone, there is little effect and differentiation, thus reducing the power of the delivery. However, the first question can be skillfully used to set up the second by reducing our rate of speech and lowering our tone: "What did you think about that?" (listen to reply, acknowledge, and then …) "And I am curious about something … how did that make you feel?" As you voice these questions as suggested, can you hear the difference in their power?

4. **We open up and explore** – A critical piece of the conversational puzzle that helps your client articulate what else is on their mind, so that you can then help them refine what is most important to them to cover in your conversation. See the later section on **agenda**.

5. **We enable high-value thinking** – We become a thinking partner who is able to bring clarity to the client's mind and help them focus on what is truly important. There is that great expression "you can't see the forest for trees," which evokes in our minds those negative feelings of being lost and confused, unsure which way to go and lacking

a clear direction. Compare that to the positive feeling of relief at the trees opening up and clear landmarks being identified that serve as beacons to the way ahead.

6. **We refine the essence** – These are the golden nuggets of our client interactions. Think about how many thousands of gallons of rushing, noisy water it takes to sluice out a single ounce of gold. Think of all the words one person can say in a one-hour conversation—potentially thousands (we've all experienced that fast-talking, motormouth salesperson, haven't we?). If you, as listener, are able to truly partner in the conversation and separate out those pieces of gold, think about the value you are bringing. Feedback from our clients, such as: "Gosh, I never even thought to look at things that way," or "looking at this from a different perspective is just so helpful," will speak to that value.

7. **We share our values** – You may recall a moment in a conversation when you felt really aligned with who you were speaking with. It's a nice, warm feeling that sometimes derives from how you both look at life or at an issue. It fundamentally builds trust in a working partnership.

   In some typical real estate training, we are taught to ask: "What criteria do you look for in a real estate professional?" and then latch on to what the client says and *talk* and *tell* to those points, essentially trying to convince the client why we are the best person for the job. Does it work? Sometimes, of course. However, another way to approach this is simply to ask your client: "I am curious ... what values are important to you in a working relationship?" This allows them to share whatever is important to them and then you can reciprocate. For example: "May I share the values that are important to me?"

Now, some of you will be thinking, *Well, that's all fine, but what if our values don't align?* That's okay—take this as a perfect opportunity to move deeper in conversation (as you'll discover in the next chapter when you take the Elevator Ride) to find out more about those values and build partnership as you go, probing and looking for commonalities to build upon. Should we work with every single client we meet, given the chance? Of course not! Just ask any veteran agent and they will give you concrete examples of clients they just could not work with. Conversely, should a client work with every single agent they meet? Of course not! The same applies. One party sometimes has to let the other go for the benefit of both; it's as simple as that. So, please do not get caught up in an illusion that you can and will work with every client, because you will only be disappointed.

How tremendously satisfying would it feel to be able to build and sustain a productive and successful business by working with clients who you enjoy quality partnerships with?

Just remember the value of true engagement. Here's an example to work through. Let's say a client lists amongst other values that: "Integrity is very important to me, so having an agent with integrity is essential." If your reply is: "Yes, integrity is also very important to me," then we are skating on the surface of value in the conversation and we are not really advancing partnership.

Instead, you could approach this with a question such as: "What is it about integrity that is important to you?" This is where we start to dig down. Let's say the answer was: "Well, the last agent we had promised us all kinds of things and failed to deliver." Would you be glad you had asked that question? You bet! It then enables you to drill down further, such as: "Thanks for sharing that—if I am your next agent, and in future you were to tell your friends that I work with great integrity, what would that look like?"

"Well, you'd have been completely up-front about the value of our home, you'd have executed all the marketing activities promised and been great to work with, I guess."

"Awesome. So, pricing your home accurately and realistically and then executing an agreed-upon marketing plan are things you are looking for in your next agent—is that about right?"

"That's about it in a nutshell."

"Great. Are you ready to have that discussion about price and marketing plans?"

"You know, let's do that. Your approach is very different to that last agent, and, to be honest, I am feeling more comfortable with you."

So, take some time to ruminate upon the values that are most important to you and which ones would be important to share with a potential client.

8. **We create a mutual win** – Personally, my sense is that the age-old expression "let's create a win–win" is best adjusted to: "let's create a mutual win," as it will help us clarify how we can work together most effectively. "A win for me and a win for you" sounds very similar to a mutual win. The key difference, from my perspective, is how we get to that *dual* win. If we embrace the concept of accomplishing it together—mutually at each step of the way, instead of each arriving there on our own—then we are creating this win as a team rather than separately. As we share values between client and agent, the key here is to take time. We are on the move from "*presentation* and *telling*" to "*conversation* and *asking*," and there is no need or reason to rush. Take time and be present. Both parties benefit.

Fundamentally, a client engagement is not like a tennis match. *Bang, bang, bang, bang, bang* … I won. It is a collaboration based upon meaningful and spontaneous client-centred interaction that better enables you as partners to move into the solution-focused phase of the working relationship.

Reconsider also the phrase "handling objections"—a classic example to me of the dated nature of some traditional sales training. Is it just me, or does that sound adversarial by nature? Doesn't it speak to a distinct possibility that there can only be one winner? It's a "come on, what else can you throw at me?" type of approach where the salesperson has an answer that eliminates every objection known to mankind in order to make the sale, instead of a powerful collaboration that focuses on the source (need) before the solution (sale).

Set your long-term intention of building a long-lasting business association, where the prize is not just the one transaction in front of you but a multitude of transactions over time that can be sourced back to this one client.

People talk about "win-win" relationships, the inference being that both parties win. Is that win equal? Maybe, maybe not. If you reframe "win-win" to "mutual win" and therefore "partners win," we can clearly see what it is we need to achieve to create that win for both parties—this Partnership Framework.

Often, clients aren't aware that there are things they don't know. Through the adoption of partnership, you will help them discover what that might be and guide them to a solution.

9. **We guide and enable client articulation** – When we are working with a client, managing a conversation is not defined by *leading* it. We often assume *control* is required and that there has to be a leader. Is that really true? Or is it more about guiding the framework of the conversation through mutual agreement? Consider how you are showing up for conversations—is it in a way

that allows all participants to bring forth what they need through a managed, guided process?

I have heard so many experienced agents say that they "feel the need"—the need to lead. You can lead the process, sure, because that's where some of your expertise lies. However, I encourage you to move with the ebb and flow of the conversational tide, and feel the need to *guide*.

So ... what if you release yourself from this urge to lead?

My hunch is that you will feel more like a conversational partner—especially when you adopt my shared agenda principle (more to come on that ... stay tuned).

10. **We release ourselves from assumptions, fear, and anticipating outcome** – There are lots of occasions in life which seem primed to make us feel nervous: examinations, job interviews, social occasions— things at which we have a very hard time not attaching ourselves to the outcome.

Your perception of having to give a speech to a large audience for the first time can take various forms, from absolute dread though to great excitement. What helps to create this predisposition? Among other things, perhaps thoughts of freezing, forgetting our words, assuming people won't understand or value our message?

A real estate agent is heading to a *listing presentation*—traditional industry terminology for an appointment with a potential client who is possibly interested in selling their property or is curious about market value. They have prepared some materials in advance and taken some preparatory steps before showing up at the house at 3:00 p.m. As their car approaches the property and they bring it to a stop, reality kicks in. For those who truly understand higher-level communication skills, these types of opportunities match their own sweet spots and they go on to have an engaging and value-filled interaction, focusing on building a great relationship and helping the client dig deep into the conversation around real estate and its impact on their life. At the other end of the spectrum, there are agents who knock on the front door and go straight into presentation mode—a kind of "okay, here's what we're going to do today" approach. They are attached to the outcome of getting the listing, plain and simple, rather than building rapport and partnering with the client. More on this later …

11. **We build mutual trust** – When we are able to reach the promised land of truly being on the proverbial same page as our client, our working relationship is comprised of trust on behalf of both parties. This could be demonstrated simply as the faith that your client will respond in a timely manner through to their complete assurance in your ability to deliver promised actions and results.

12. **We engage and work together with confidence** – Confidence is a key ingredient in partnership. It underlays everything that we do. As with trust, it

is a two-way element: both parties aligning with confidence.

Let's call these our "Twelve Principles of Partnership." Ask yourself, "What will happen to my client relationships if I am able to live these?"

What if you reflect on the level of partnership with your clients? Think about a client you are currently working with.

- What do you notice about the conversations you typically have?
- How would you assess your level of partnership with that client, based on these twelve principles?
- What can you identify as a personal development growth area?

The client and me, together – Again, reflect on your current client relationships, and ask yourself:

- How are we showing up together?
- What typical interactions—our norms—are at play presently?
- Have I checked in with my clients to evaluate the quality of our working partnerships?

Unless your business contemplates steamrolling its way through business relationships, or if you just cannot get your head around an alternative, modern way of engagement in sales, partnership is of fundamental importance to master. **What happens if you replace the traditional "How can I help you today?" that suggests "I am going to advise you" with wording like: "What would you like to get out of our conversation today?" This simple** introduction speaks to the very essence of partnership and is a great starting point to setting the interaction up for its greatest chance of success.

Eight essential elements of thought-provocation

There is a four-word response that indicates you are doing a proficient job in this area: "That's a great question." We have all thought it or said it aloud when someone asked something that moved us deeper in our thinking. Thought-provoking questions have very powerful effects and play a key part in the coaching experience.

Here are eight essential elements of thought-provocation that really stand out for me. **When we provoke thought, we ...**

1. **Arouse a feeling or encourage the start of an action** – We talked about engaging mind and heart in section 2 of the partnership summary. It is

very much applicable to the process of provoking thought as well.

2. **We stimulate deeper thinking** – "Hmm, good question; I am going to have to think that through ..." shares with us the indication that deeper thought will ensue.

3. **We encourage self-reflection** – Like cogs in an engine, the wheels of thought are in motion as we pause to think.

4. **We can trigger key developmental thinking** – Especially satisfying is the provoking question that elicits a response indicating that an idea has been born, evidenced by a response such as: "You know, I have just thought of something ..."

5. **We challenge existing assumptions** – We all have them! We walk around with them. Our negative mind says, "I know what this buyer is going to be like" or "I know this seller won't likely list with me."

A potential buyer says to their agent, "We really want a house, but we can only afford a condo. We don't believe a condo would work for us with young kids, so we'll just continue renting this house ..." Where would some agents take this conversation? Nowhere—they assume that this buyer is not going to buy, so decide to move on the next "real" buyer. Meantime, the buyer meets a fantastic agent who truly partners with her and, during early conversations, carefully invites the client to challenge her assumption. "What if you were to look at this differently? What if the four of you lived in a condo and didn't have to worry about the upkeep of a house and yard ... how could that actually benefit your lifestyle?" **As consumers, we often don't really know what we want.** We have an idea and some urgent, as yet unrefined, thoughts to the future. This is where we can really add value as agents, if we just stop and think about it. People need guidance, from the birth of the idea of purchasing all the way through to actually buying.

6. **We open the possibility to actually change** – Along with challenging underlying assumptions, we have the ability to promote a conversational environment that encourages an openness to change. Most of us fall into a rut or period of inaction from time to time. You can really help a client take on the responsibility for making change by promoting this openness. For example, you ask them, "On a scale of one to ten, how open are you to making change?" The client responds with, "Let's say a six or seven." You then ask, "I am curious ... what would need to happen for that to be a nine or a ten?" "Well, I guess I need be more decisive about making some changes in my life, get off the chair and actually go and speak with a mortgage broker and then get out and look at some places."

If we encourage our clients to identify and define specific actions that they need to take (in other words, coming up with their own solutions with some competent guidance from you), then we are aligning with them beautifully, simply by provoking their thoughts about making change and pondering what impact those changes could have on their lives.

7. **We learn to harness the power of silence and space** – Ask yourself, how comfortable are you at holding a period of silence within a conversation? You've just asked that great question and your client is pondering. This is where the magic happens! Avoid jumping in at all costs. Avoid adding in any more words to the question. We do not need any more noise. Hold the space. Look at your notepad or gaze away at something. By allowing the time and silent space for your client to contemplate a question, we are likely building and delivering value. (This is a high-value skill—more on it later.)

8. **We encourage vision through a different lens** – For example, let's say you are having a conversation about price with a seller whose property has been on the market for a long time, and who believes that the worth of their property is in a different realm than what all the feedback from actual active buyers is suggesting. A simple yet powerful question that illustrates this change of lens is: "What if you were to look at your price through the eyes of a buyer? Let's see what other choices they have and any challenges they might see in your property ..."

Thought-provoking questions are vital in helping your clients refine what they hope to achieve. Picture yourself standing next to your client on the platform of a train station. There are lots of journeys and destinations possible—how can you help guide them toward the most appropriate one? If you can be the agent who encourages different trains of thought and helps in determining the best route to take, won't you be valued for that?

Six essential elements of being creative

Do you consider yourself a creative person? When I ask this question to small groups of people, I'd estimate that only about a quarter of the group will raise their hands. Indeed, I never used to think of myself as being creative—never good at artwork, could barely draw a stick man, so that must have meant I was not really creative.

Simply by reframing the question to become open-ended, like: "In what ways would you consider yourself a creative person?" (and therefore landing a more thought-provoking question), I can come up with ways that definitely qualify me as being creative, such as having a passion for creating a garden landscape and growing plants and vegetables, as well as for specific choices of words and language to use in dialogue. How creative are you?

What happens when we *create*?

1. **We can bring something out of the dark and into the light** – By being creative, we can draw something out of someone that they are unable to see themselves. Talk about adding value in a way that most others would not even think about!

2. **We can encourage a new behaviour or action** – For example: "The property is not showing very well; as there is so much furniture and belongings in the upstairs rooms, they look smaller than they really are. What effect could it have if we were to de-clutter and re-arrange everything?"

3. **We can elicit options and alternatives** – Through a dialogue around different possibilities and examining things from a "what if" perspective. An example would be drawing out from your buyer several different scenarios, in case their first-choice location or property is not an available or financially plausible option.

4. **We can provide an open, safe, trusting environment** – When we are in creative mode, how do we feel? Normally, we feel positive and in a state of achievement. This builds on the two-way trust established as a quality of partnership and encourages creative thinking.

5. **We can cause something to actually happen** – We move away from the status quo and start to make

a shift in behaviour, announcing that a potential change is actually in motion. When we are in a slower real estate market, we wonder if a property will ever sell, if some buyers will ever make a decision. The ability to create a shift in behaviour can make the difference that will make a seller actually sell or a buyer actually buy. Which, after all, is their goal, isn't it?

Buyers sitting on the fence in slower markets and sellers sitting tight on asking prices are examples of scenarios where we can be really creative and draw out from them a different perspective that actually causes something to happen—like an offer or a lowering of price.

6. **We can provide new perspectives** – What happens when we pick up a pair of binoculars? Typically, we are met with a view that is out of focus, so we adjust one eye and then the other. Only then can we enjoy a better perspective of what we are looking at. In life, we all walk around with our own view of the world. It is limited and seen from our unique perspective. When someone says back to you, "You know, I have never looked at the issue like that before … now it is starting to make sense," you are given feedback that you have managed to draw out a new and refreshed perspective. This is very similar to encouraging sight through a different lens. There is high-potential value in helping our clients see something through a different window, through a different lens, or from a different angle.

Many successful salespeople pride themselves on being creative solution providers—which is very valuable, make no mistake. In terms of further skill development, what if this is enhanced by having your clients become creative partners with you, through which solutions emerge from the brilliance of the questions you ask, the observations you make, and the guiding role you play?

As we get to the decisions that need to be made, eliciting client-generated solutions and strategies is our best path, as the client has full ownership of them. The quality of questions you ask to encourage and challenge these solutions is critical to ensure that these solutions and strategies are valid to your client, always keeping in mind the specifics of their personal real estate circumstances.

Eight essential elements of inspiration

Following on from all this creativity, we have the opportunity to truly inspire.

What happens when we *inspire*?

1. **We reduce our clients' self-doubt and reassure them** – When we carry around self-doubt about an issue, it creates an obstacle to progress. Do you recall that feeling of saying to someone, "Oh, I feel much better about this now," and a sense of inner calmness and relief settles in? It's a valuable component in any conversation to building trust and having confidence to take action.

2. **We stimulate their motivations and help build capability** – Motivation is a key driver in many of life's scenarios. In real estate, its importance is paramount. The less motivation a buyer or seller has, the harder it is to help them achieve an objective. Inspiration provides a motivational quality, and builds belief in competency development. Being able to inspire someone requires many different elements: professional presence, trust, background knowledge, depth of previous conversations, and so on. If you can help build a client's competency to reach a goal, then you're adding real value.

3. **We enhance their thinking process** – When we feel inspired, our minds tend to open, and we can think and dream freely. For example, how do we feel if we are physically active and then watch the Olympics? We feel even more inspired to set goals, try harder, be consistent in our fitness actions. We hear incredibly inspirational stories of athletes overcoming serious injuries and setbacks, yet being inspired by those before them to aim for the podium. In slower markets, when both buyers and sellers seem to be inactive, think about how you

can enhance their thoughts and inspire action. I believe you'll love the perspectives on this later on, in section eight ...

4. **We help them to paint a picture** – "A picture is worth a thousand words" aptly describes the power of visuality. If we are able to inspire someone to create a picture of their future, their dreams, their goals, they will likely become more engaged and aligned in the conversation, and will participate at a higher level of partnership. A fabulous example of this as it relates to working with a buyer is the traditional "needs analysis" performed by most agents, which starts out focused on solutions rather than source. Let's be clear: there needs to be that analysis; the opportunity here is to understand the effect of adding in an inspirational element to the conversation. So, here's an example of agent and client in discussion:

"What are you looking for?"

"A two-bedroom condo on a higher floor, hopefully a nice kitchen, 700+ square feet, maybe no older than ten years, in the downtown core in our price range."

"Great, I am pretty clear on what you need now. Let me do some research and then we can head out on Saturday to look at some suites, okay?"

Now compare this to an agent in conversation who understands the part inspiration can play....

"What are you looking for?"

"A two-bedroom condo on a higher floor, hopefully a nice kitchen, 700+ square feet, maybe no older than ten years, in the downtown core in our price range."

"That sounds exciting—let's have a bit of fun with this. Imagine you are walking out of the elevator and opening the front door to your new home ... what is in there?"

"There's a good-sized living room, the kitchen has one of those bars in granite that we can sit at and eat ... the deck is big enough to have barbeques ... there's a gleaming hardwood floor ... the ensuite bathroom has a tub and shower—it feels like our home!"

"Thanks for sharing. How are you feeling as you visualize your next home?"

"I can't wait to move in! It sounds so much better than where we are renting. Do you think we can find that in our price range?"

"I am really looking forward to taking this journey with you. We are a team working together to get as close as we can to your vision. Let me do some research and then we can head out on Saturday to look at some suites, okay?"

Which version builds better partnership? Of course, this does not apply to every situation, but it is a great tool to have in your kit to bring out when you need to make that difference.

5. **We can skillfully coax out something important** – This is a particular asset that being able to inspire someone brings into play: the ability to actually draw something out of someone through *asking* instead of *advising* and *telling*. **Questions provide answers. *Telling* does not.** It's back to the classic client query: "What do you think I should do?" If we always respond to this question by *telling* instead of *asking*, we reduce our ability to draw forth key challenges or thoughts.

6. **We energize and bring fresh positivity** – When we discuss options and actively create forward-thinking, how do we generally feel? We come to life, we become more engaged in the conversation, and may even feel a sense of growth. How do we as humans feel when someone says to us, "Wow, you are so passionate about what you are doing." We feel an enhanced sense of purpose and alignment with ourselves and our self-worth. We feel alive! Reflect on how you energize your clients and enliven their spirits—are you doing that as well as possible?

7. **We produce alignment of mind and heart** – Under "Partnership," we identified the idea of engaging both mind and heart: "When we are able to encourage a client's thoughts and emotions in combination, we take them to a place they might not find on their own." If that combination occurs and becomes an alignment, then the power of inspiration will be in full flow. We can tap into their passion to achieve and positively combine their thoughts with their feelings. When we don't feel good about the decisions we make, we feel at

cross purposes and misaligned. Conversely, when we feel good about the decisions we make, we feel aligned and inspired.

8. **We can engage them with valuable storytelling** – At times when we feel at a loss and not particularly confident about the future in general or about a certain issue in particular, hearing a story of success from people in a similar situation can be highly inspirational. In hot markets, where demand far exceeds supply, buyers who have come second or lower in many multiple-offer situations can be extremely disheartened and negative about the whole experience—understandably so. So how can we possibly inspire them?

"Bob and Mary, I am aware we have lost out on three successive properties. How are you feeling?"

"We seriously feel like giving up. It seems impossible to buy anything; there's no light at the end of the tunnel."

"May I share with you a real-life story of clients of mine in a similar situation and how it all worked out fine in the end?"

"I guess so, though we seem to have no luck at all."

"Thank you. Another couple I was working with moved into their new home just last month. They had lost out in about seven or eight previous multiple-offer negotiations. They felt exactly the same as you yet stuck with it and were successful. I am here for you; we will make it happen. The key here is patience. This market asks a lot of all of us; it is ever so challenging, but I am sure we will find you a fantastic property."

Who doesn't love to hear an inspiring speaker at an event? Inspiration is such a wonderful quality to offer. As an ICF-recognized professional coach, my job is to inspire clients to maximize their personal and professional potential, and time and again I see how important inspiration is.

Four essential results of boosting potential

Now that you have partnered, provoked, created, and inspired, you'll find that the opportunity to maximize potential has been generated. Potential is a big, limitless kind of word. It speaks to things that might be within the realm of possibility but have not yet been achieved. As children, we have enormous potential, and boundaries only seem to emerge as we travel through life and make choices. Yet, no matter where we are and what we are doing, potential is ever-present and refreshes itself as the sun rises each day.

Nearly all of us have limits we place on ourselves, ceilings under which we feel we should operate. We create boundaries as to what we can do and cannot do.

As we round out this section, here are four results of boosting potential:

1. **Currently unrealized competence can be tapped into** – Think about something you have achieved in your life that at first seemed highly unlikely. Personally, I remember getting into an elevator after my first half-marathon in Seattle. I had run it as hard as I could and finished in around one hour and thirty-eight minutes. I was exhausted. As the doors closed and the elevator started rising, I said out loud to myself, "How on earth do people run a full marathon?" I was thinking about how it is twice as far as I had just run—another twenty-one kilometres—and how I was feeling absolutely tapped out. In effect, I was placing that ceiling on my own potential in that moment.

   The following year, I completed by first marathon in three hours and thirty minutes. I had tapped into my own unrealized ability.

   Some marathon runners go on to ultra-marathons and a few go way beyond that. They are the ones truly tapping into their full potential in that arena. I tapped into some of mine.

I believe most of us fail to realize our full potential due to lack of motivation, know-how, awareness, or many other factors. Real estate as a career is just the same—that often-quoted saying that 10 percent of the agents make 90 percent of the revenues. Conversely, 90 percent of agents share that tiny 10 percent slice of revenues.

Think about the potential you have in this career. The income potential does not have a cap or ceiling on it—it is possible to keep on earning without restriction. That is a big part of what attracts so many new licensees each year, seconded by the perception of flexibility and the ability to manage one's own time. So, we have this dichotomy:

-   No income limitations, ability and flexibility to manage one's own time without a boss
-   Only 10 percent share 90 percent of revenues

There are all types of prescriptive training courses out there, and every one of them offers value of one sort or another. Having been directly involved in this industry over several decades, I have mused on why the ratios are what they are and the career failure rate so high.

And my conclusion matches the elevator panel you will see in our next chapter: **most agents are looking for that solution-based magic formula that they hope to implement from someone else instead of looking within themselves and searching through what is lurking down in the depths of their persona before moving forward and taking action**.

An example of unrealized ability: We decide we are on a quest to get in shape. We want to be leaner, more muscular, more energetic. What is involved in that objective? For many, it is actually going to the gym, exercising aerobically and lifting weights. We look over and see someone else who ticks all the boxes of what we might consider "in shape." They have the physique we yearn for yet cannot get close to. Sure, genetics and other factors play a role, but the point is that most of us do not commit to all of the factors necessary toward fulfilling the potential of our objective: a proper sleep routine, a better diet, when and how often we exercise. We are happy that we got to the gym two to three times in the week and are feeling pretty good about it.

What about boosting potential for our clients? A common case here might be the buyer who wants to live centrally yet is priced out to a market away from their desired area. They had their heart set on a downtown condo, and prices have dictated that reality requires a shift in thinking—see below.

2. **Capacity to do can be brought into the sunshine** – This is a big one! How much of our vast individual potential do we actually develop into substance? How many of us truly get the most out of our enormous individual capacity? As licensees, do we know what we are capable of? The answer in most cases is *no*! The serious producers do not share that self-doubt, they design systems that they can rely on to help their clients reach their objectives, and as a result their own. The focus is on the journey, not the destination. They are not self-limiting their

capacity and typically share a belief that they can grow it to perform better business by growth, often through building a team. They bring their careers into the sunshine.

3. **Shifts in beneficial thinking and behaviour come to the fore** – We talked earlier about "causing something to happen," and, with inspiration, this is where shifts can occur and move to the front of our thinking. Taking action is what happens when we understand and acknowledge that we have unrealized ability and commit to searching out our potential.

For our clients, the realization that perhaps a central downtown market is no longer a viable option has been extremely disappointing. The vision they had for their lives requires some adjustments. How can you help with that?

As an example, let's examine an area called the River District in Vancouver. A sleepier market for years, Fraserlands was not considered very central and so it wasn't typically in the running for most buyers. More recently, with the expansion to the River District, the whole area has become very popular for buyers who recognize the pleasure of living by the Fraser River and not having to cross any bridges into town. It's unlikely most of these buyers *started* their search there.

Real estate agents are more mobile than ever, and the knowledge base for most of us now includes multiple markets—the escalation in prices has seen their clientele move into many different neighbourhoods of the market.

So, how can we help our clients make a shift in behaviour? For example, let's say it is a very expensive but quiet buyer's market. Three such scenarios might be:

- For buyers, perhaps a change of focus to a market that they can afford.
- For buyers, making an offer in a range that is acceptable to sellers rather than remaining too low.
- For sellers, pricing their homes at levels that attract viewers and enable offers.

In all three scenarios, the quality of the professional relationship and the establishment of the Partnership Framework will enhance an agent's ability to help their client make a shift in behaviour and decision.

4. **Possibilities of outcome can be identified and planned for** – After you have established a partnership dialogue with lots of thought-provocation, creativity, and inspiration, the starting line for whatever subject you are discussing can come into sight.

You know what it's like when you've been stuck in the woods for ages and suddenly see a clear plain ahead? Or, you've been climbing steadily up a mountainside to reach a ridge and suddenly the summit comes into full view? For an agent, this might be a decisive moment for a client to make change and commit to setting goals and paths to reach them (or for them as agents to do the same for their own businesses).

As we boost potential for our clients, we help them to see what is achievable. Agent to client: "Let's imagine for a moment that we have the moving truck full and it has left the house. Everything has been cleaned and you are ready to hand over the keys to the buyer. You're ready to embark on that next stage of life. How is that feeling?"

"I feel a huge sense of relief. Some sadness to be leaving the house after so long, but excited to start life in a new location. Yes, it feels great!"

"Thanks for sharing that. What do you see as the next steps for us to bring that vision to life?"

"I guess we need to plan out getting the house ready to go on the market."

"That makes sense. What would be the first thing on your list to do?"

The agent then guides her client through a discovery of steps that the client himself identifies as being appropriate to preparing the house for sale. These are client-generated solutions that are owned by the client.

In our everyday real estate conversations, we come into contact with people who are either starting or thinking of starting a journey of discovery, or are somewhere along that journey's path. From experience, what we know is that it is rare to move ahead in linear fashion; most such journeys involve a number of twists and turns along the way, and this is where our client coaching can be of the most value in building working partnerships through to realizing potential for your client. But there's more ...

A journey to take together

Finally, consider this for a moment. We have five key terms in our partnership framework: partner, thought-provoke, create, inspire, and potential.

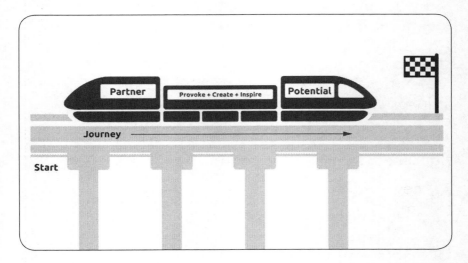

What happens when we take the first and last words, *partner* and *potential*, and look at them as the engines of our powerful conversational locomotive? Do you see what I see? When we partner together, setting out on a journey that flows through to a successful conclusion and possession of a property, we actually **maximize potential for both partners**. We mutually achieve our objectives by working together. The client fulfills their objective and takes delivery of a new property, while we fulfill ours of helping them and we are remunerated for that. And here's the key: the higher the quality of that working relationship, the better chance for repeat and referral business—and perhaps a career ambassador for life who can play an important role in recommending others to you for wonderful service.

How about some self-discovery? Are you willing to commit to the Partnership Framework? Is it a great place to start by having that conversation with yourself, to understand how these principles show up for you, before you exercise them on your clients?

Summary of core principles and self-reflection

Our learning objectives were to understand:
- **What the Partnership Framework is**
- **What the five keys words mean in our context.**
- **What actually happens when we partner, provoke thought, create, inspire, and boost potential.**

Now is an opportunity to reflect on how the Partnership Framework can apply in the work you do. How can you reframe and refine how you interact with your clients?

To help you contemplate this, here are some good questions to ask yourself as good reference points:

Operational mode:
Do you lead or guide? Do you aim to lead conversations, or guide them?

Source or solution? Is your default to be the provider of solutions, or do you typically strive to help your clients gain a better understanding of what surrounds an objective before helping them formulate their own solutions?

Tell or ask? Is your tendency to answer all the questions you face? Are you typically the provider of answers and opinions, or do you tend to collaborate and ask your clients lots of meaningful questions to help them think clearly?

Either before or during meetings (or both!), do you regularly make assumptions?

Conversational mode:
How creative are your conversations?

Do your conversations stimulate deeper developmental thinking for others?

What's behind the scenes for you?
What outcome do you normally attach yourself to—and does that actually help?

Do you inspire people?

What fears lurk invisibly behind your conversations?

Do you position yourself to help others reach their potential?

What action steps within your control are required to stimulate powerful conversations and help enact meaningful change and better empowered client decisions?

Are you on the way to building deeper, more effective working relationships with your clients?

Section 2

The Elevator Ride to Successful Partnership Communication

When we set ourselves and our clients up in "presentation mode," we tend to impose limitations on the potential of both the immediate conversation and the longer-term working relationship. How can we better frame out our working relationship and mutually fulfill its potential?

Learning objectives are to understand:
- **How to use the Elevator Ride to connect with your clients**
- **The eleven Core Competencies of the International Coach Federation**
- **How ICF defines the responsibilities of a coach**
- **What coaching actually is (and is *not*)**
- **The importance of curiosity**
- **The relevance of reframing your conversations and making a conscious shift in how you approach them**

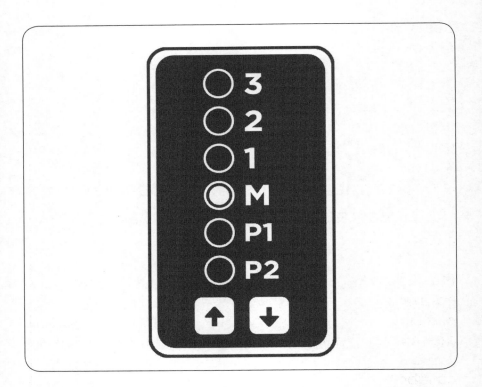

Connecting through the Elevator Ride, not the elevator pitch!

Take a good long look at this image. The design was inspired by a curious desire to see how agents would interpret it. Yes, it is designed to resemble an elevator panel. Over many classes, I have heard a wide variety of different interpretations of what it might signify—anything from "it's a four-storey building with two levels of parking beneath" to "we're stuck on the main floor and don't know where to go." Then thoughts begin to percolate, and I start to hear things like "the arrows indicate choice; it is possible to move up or down, or stay where we are." As the thinking in the room progresses, I hear "if we dig down deeper, we can find out what our clients want to achieve" or "this is like an emotional elevator—it describes the up and down emotions involved in a real estate transaction."

This image forms the essence of what I term the Partnership Framework. As agents, **we are often so focused on providing solutions as quickly as we can that we lose a massive opportunity to cement a powerful partnership with a client, one that might endure for years and result in multiple transactions together.**

Are you still wondering about the difference between this Elevator Ride and an elevator pitch?

The Elevator Ride invites a mutual and spontaneous partnership in inquiry, reflection, and discovery; by its very nature, a typical elevator pitch is presentation-based, descriptive, persuasive, and pre-planned. Which one do you believe offers the best opportunity to engage and collaborate with a real estate buyer or seller?

Back to the image. My own interpretation is that level 3 is the solution—the point at which a buyer makes a decision to work with you, possibly signing an exclusive agreement to do so, or a seller makes a decision to proceed and sign a listing contract with you.

Another example of reaching level 3 is when a buyer makes a buying decision, or a seller makes a selling decision, and they proceed to a final conclusion.

In both cases, levels 1 and 2 are action steps towards the solution. As such, I call the levels above M the "solutions-based" phase.

P1 and P2 are where the real opportunities lie—both to build a deep relationship based on situational or objective-driven analysis and to further differentiate yourself. This area is what we'll refer to as the "person-based phase," where, instead of focusing merely on solutions and solution-based lines of questioning, we actually assume a role similar to that of a professional coach, where we help our clients uncover their true motivations, hopes, fears, concerns, dreams, values, and beliefs. We do this by helping them gain a better understanding of exactly what they want to accomplish, the impacts of doing so, and anything else that is relevant to the decisions that will need to be made.

What if we embrace this elevator imagery and learn how to frame our conversational engagements in ways that differentiate between the solution-based phase and the person-based phase, and in doing so build an understanding of where you are together on the Elevator Ride? How would that enable you to stand out? How different is that in essence to an elevator pitch? How valuable would that be to your clients? And how valuable could that be for your career? My hope is that you'll become more reflective and self-aware, and be able to bring this image to mind as you engage in conversation with your past, present, and future clients.

So, if we call level M up to 3 *solution-based* and level M down to P2 *person-based*, it is interesting to dwell for a moment on P1 and P2. Could those be the locomotive engines again that we referred to at the end of the first section, *partner* and *potential*? Our industry norm is predominantly to head up to 3—using mostly solution-based questions— and thinking that this will yield the best result in terms of potential. Yet, if we make a concerted effort to head down into P1 and P2, we are focusing instead on the person—the client—and I believe this will actually increase the quality of our partnership and its potential!

Understanding the eleven Core Competencies of the International Coach Federation

As you start contemplating the Elevator Ride and thinking about how you might reframe your conversations, let me introduce you to a short summary of the eleven ICF Core Competencies, together with my own words to describe their value and meaning in a real estate sales context.

Personally, these competencies have had a substantial impact on my career by helping me to develop and drive deeper, broader, and more impactful conversations. My natural tendency has always leaned towards curiosity and to taking a coaching approach to conversation. As I look back, it was the discovery of ICF and subsequent professional credentialing through their system that fundamentally propelled me forward and played a significant part in inspiring me to bring change to this industry; best of all, change which I believe is sustainable into the future and which will build and offer value for all.

These principles are grouped into four main categories: Setting the Foundation, Co-Creating the Relationship, Communicating Effectively, and Facilitating Learning and Results. One of the big inspirations for writing this book was the realization that these eleven competencies apply so well to real estate sales,

Setting the Foundation

1. **Meeting ethical guidelines and professional standards** – What is required of a coach is similar

to what real estate client relationships look like, in so many ways.

2. **Establishing the coaching agreement** – The ability to understand what is required in the spontaneous conversations with your clients.

Co-Creating the Relationship
3. **Establishing trust and intimacy with the client** – Being able to create a supportive and safe environment that embraces mutual respect and trust.

4. **Coaching presence** – How you are showing up and building value through spontaneous conversation that is open and confident, and truly being present to what your client requires.

Communicating Effectively
5. **Active listening** – Understanding the different listening choices; taking in what is or is not being said and supporting your clients in determining and expressing what is important to them.

6. **Powerful questioning** – Developing the ability to dig deep in order to help you and your clients move forward together.

7. **Direct communication** – Spontaneously employing language that has the greatest positive impact on your clients.

Facilitating Learning and Results
8. **Creating awareness** – Helping your clients to be aware of what is most important to them and what surrounds every decision they make, and

integrating this all together to help move forward and achieve results.

9. **Designing actions** – Assisting your clients to realize what is needed and then to describe actions that will speak to their desired results.

10. **Planning and goal setting** – The ability to develop and maintain an effective listing or buying plan of action with your clients.

11. **Managing progress and accountability** – Being there to guide progress, keep your clients focused, and hold them accountable and responsible to take any actions required.

As you review each one, let it sink in and reflect on how important it is. Every one of them can be applied to our client relationships. Look how relevant they are: numbers 2, 4, and 8 stand out in their importance in finding out what someone wants to achieve and how you show up to help them achieve it. Note the depth of skill required to reach mastery of 5, 6, and 7, and then the bringing-it-all-home aspects of actual results in 9, 10, and 11.

What are the four responsibilities of the coach, as defined by the ICF?

- Discover, clarify, and align with what the client wants to achieve
- Encourage client self-discovery
- Elicit client-generated solutions and strategies
- Hold the client responsible and accountable

That last one is often challenging for agents to grasp, and I often hear, "We are holding the client accountable?"

Indeed. Ultimately, our clients are responsible for making decisions on pricing and offers. Don't lose sight of that. If you feel you are the only one who is accountable, then there is probably a weaker partnership happening than is evident on the surface.

Here's a question: in great working relationships, should the decisions clients make align with their *original* goals? That depends on a variety of factors, including market conditions and needs or motivations that might change along the way. **The one thing we can safely say is that the more we have partnered with our client, the higher the likelihood of them being happy with their final decisions**. If the requirement goalposts change during the business relationship, your job is to adapt to those changes. So, integrating these four clear responsibilities into your tool chest will enable you to operate on an exciting new level.

Let's take a closer look:

Discover, clarify, and align with what the client wants to achieve – Fundamentally, our business is built upon helping our client achieve their real estate visions and objectives. Plain and simple, it is helping them with that discovery process at the beginning, lifting the fog of uncertainty or challenge, and partnering in alignment with what they set out to accomplish.

Encourage client self-discovery – The more a client can understand all that surrounds and influences the decisions they make, the better the chance of those decisions being solid. If we play the role of guide at its fullest potential, we are able to draw out those self-discoveries. Think of it this way: we are the experts in real estate, while they are the experts in their own life.

Elicit client-generated solutions and strategies – We know by now the immense power of client-generated solutions that come through a robust coaching approach.

Hold the client responsible and accountable – As mentioned above, enable accountability to the decisions the client makes and key parts of the process within their control.

If we can therefore agree that the ICF responsibilities mirror those of a real estate agent, doesn't it therefore provide further validity to the Partnership Framework?

Now that we have discovered the four big pieces of the puzzle (Partnership Framework, Elevator Ride, ICF Core Competencies, and Coach Responsibilities) let's take a deep dive into how we see coaching at first glance …

How real estate agents interpret what coaching means

I love to start my group coaching work by dividing the agents into two small groups and asking them to write up words that they believe are solid descriptors for the word "coaching," a simple question that has garnered a surprising range of answers. It is a great way to immediately start the learning, and the range of responses points to what I had originally thought: that the word "coaching" is often misinterpreted and misunderstood. While many of the skills involved are easily identified, other words suggested as descriptors for coaching are actually misaligned. Over time, and with input from over 150 agents with a full range of tenure and experience in our business, this sample group have provided over 100 words that, to them, align with their understanding of coaching.

What I particularly appreciate about this exercise is the opportunity it creates to fast-track the learning and open the mind to new ideas. In support of that, I have grouped many of the answers into three categories:

A – these are what, to me, coaching is all about
B – these speak to the essence of coaching, but require some distinct clarity
C – these are actually *not* what coaching is all about.

I used to be involved with youth soccer, and ran a few small teams while my own kids were little. I used to show them how to kick and trap a ball, how to score goals, how to defend, how to be a good teammate, and so on. What makes this most challenging is that society calls that role a coach. In some ways it is, in terms of inspiring, challenging, building competency, and so forth. In another, it was actually showing how to do things— mentoring. Let's immerse ourselves in words that have come to mind when contemplating coaching:

A – These words are what coaching is all about, in terms of the recipient of the coaching (the client):

Empowering – a wonderful gift to give them

Accountability – helping someone determine who and what they want to be accountable for

Caring – creating a genuine space to fundamentally help someone

Patience – we don't rush in; we take our time

Guidance – walking together on a journey

Listening – for what's said or not actually said to inform our understanding and then be able to ask relevant questions

Communication – the higher the quality of dialogue, the greater chance of developing desired results

Assessment – helping someone identify what they can and cannot see

Constructive feedback – sharing observations; helping someone see their challenges and possibilities

Partnership – truly working together as a team

Re-direction – encouraging realignment of thought

Learning opportunity – self-reflection is a powerful enabler to learn about ourselves

Inspiration – building on positive feelings

Building trust and relationships – trust within the relationship is itself a core competency

Self-improvement – understanding that willingness needs to be in place

Powerful questioning – asking simple, thought-provoking questions to bring clarity to thought

Open-mindedness – willingness to look through another lens

Awareness – finding out what else is in the surrounding picture

Commitment – discovering action that the client can proactively commit to

Drive – understanding what motivational drivers exist or are absent

Personality assessment – understanding themselves better

Elevating performance – uncovering a desire and willingness

Behavioural change – a shift in thinking and action

Shift in perspective – viewing things from a different angle

Focusing efforts – refining the challenge through questions

Making people feel heard – accurate listening is critical

Goal orientation – determining what *they* want to get out of the conversation

Goal-setting – letting the client establish their own clear path to their goals

Finding success – guiding them on that journey

Self-assessment and awareness – asking clients to reflect and assess from their perspective

Self-reflection – past behaviours can give clues to how to deal with the future

Support – guiding them through their journey

Respect – holding space for the client and their dialogue

Offering different perspectives – facilitating the viewing of their topic from another angle

Encouraging – moving the conversation along as required

Motivating – a deep dive to find their driving motives

Tapping into different thought processes – again, perspective change or paradigm shift

Collaborating – working together through contributive conversation

Identifying vulnerabilities – a key to finding out underlying challenges, threats, or weaknesses

Sharing – trusting each other enough to share without restriction

Connecting – working within a bond that develops with ethical guidelines

Engaging – the sharing of a purpose

Uncovering strengths – helping them see and acknowledge their strengths

Developing strengths – helping identify and facilitate those steps as needed

Discovering self-limitations – the root of what may be holding them back

Action planning – key step in drawing out the actual step-by-step process of moving forward

Prompting – key thought development

Guiding to goals – walking alongside them, not leading

Listening and understanding – key elements that enable great questions

Pushing out of comfort zone – with a willing client, this can help enact powerful change

Helping develop qualities – identifying strengths and challenges, for example

Honesty – the foundation of client success

Authentic – keeping things real and true

Confidentiality –required by professional guidelines

Mutual understanding – co-developed with you both on the same page

Compassion – enabling empathy—a great quality in coaching

Expression – client expression is key

Challenging – causing shifts in required behaviour to happen, for example

Uplifting – taking the weight of issues away

Unpacking – that great ability to help someone unpack everything surrounding a challenge or goal

Digging deeper – depth provides perspective and identifies root issues or drivers

Adapting – making adjustments

Accepting change – depending on the situation, acceptance of certain pieces is critical

B – These words speak to the essence of coaching, but require some distinct clarity:

Experience – drawing out their past experiences

Support – being a guide

Measuring – how do *they* measure success rather than how you do

Messaging – the ability to draw out the right messaging rather than giving it

Contract – established between the coach and coachee—what the coachee wants to contract for

Action – client decides the actions, not the coach

Leadership – Careful! It is not where you want the conversation to go—walk alongside as a guide rather than ahead as a leader

Problem solving – drawing out problems that your client can then identify

Interactive learning – not *telling* or *instructing*

Strategizing – care around who is developing strategy

Analysis – What can the client see?

Practise – drawing out what actions the client needs to practise

Inclusion – whatever agenda your client has cannot be ignored

Discipline – helping them stay focused through the process

Structure – providing the framework (through competencies we are learning here)

Teamwork – building confidence with role clarity

Sharing knowledge – With permission! Avoid prescribing and pronouncing

Discussing plans – that the client wants to develop or refine

Participating (roles) – encouraging and inspiring conversation, not giving opinions

Friendship – establishing a healthy bond, at a respectful distance

Having fun – keeping conversation light and engaging, but reading what they need

Disciplining – helping your client create actions to be accountable to

C – These are what coaching is *not* about (unless otherwise stipulated by the client):

Instruction – a coach is not an instructor in any capacity

Educating/teaching – it is a self-educating process, not one in which you educate them

Training – you are not a trainer in a coaching conversation, you do not *tell* them anything

Skill training – only in the sense that you contract to elicit skills, but they must be client-generated

Imparting wisdom and knowledge – nope

Learning scripts – unless self-generated by the client, these are not authentic

Mentoring – showing how to do something

Leading – to be avoided, as it is not your agenda

Advising – same as mentoring, this comes later in the conversation

Leading by example – it is not about you, although you might share a story with permission

Directing – again, not your agenda

Filterer – raising awareness rather than imposing a filter on a conversation

Constructive, truthful, and positive criticism – there is no place for criticism

As you review the lists and see into which category I have slotted them, what is coming up for you? What are you seeing that challenges your traditional thinking and provides the greatest clarity and impact for you and your professional work?

Are you naturally curious?

Children constantly feel the need to investigate. As parents, it sometimes seems their little questions are endless, with a favourite being the "are we nearly there?" on long road trips. They have a thirst for knowledge and answers, and pretty much every question is natural and genuinely inquisitive. Why, why, and more why!

As adults, where does that rampant curiosity that we ourselves enjoyed as children go? Does it simply disappear? I don't believe so. My interpretation of what happens is that as our lives become more challenging and complicated over time, and we become providers instead of receivers, there are real things on the line: expenses to cover, bills to pay, goals to reach, things we yearn for and hope to be able to afford. Along with this, we experience sensations of pressure, we have expectations for ourselves, we need to make things happen. Somehow that gets translated into more *telling* than *asking*—perhaps it is because this is what many sales industries have taught their people for years and years: go and present. As discussed earlier, agents work for hours putting together a sometimes-beautiful document that is chock full of great things. Some of them arrive to meet the potential client armed with this masterpiece and get ready to present it. The mindset is: "Here's how I am going to present today."

Think what happens when we do not exercise curiosity. When we aren't curious...

1. we don't listen,
2. we are unable to have an open-minded point of view,
3. we don't bother asking questions,
4. we tell, judge, criticize, blame, and shame.

These are assertions made in Kathy Taberner and Kirsten Taberner Siggins's *The Power of Curiosity*, a must-read resource around the realm of conversations. Powerful stuff indeed—just take a few moments for that list to sink in and to fathom just how important curiosity is. I amongst others call it **natural curiosity**, as once we have naturally incorporated this skill into who we are and how we interact, it can happen naturally ... just like when we were children. The magic that can be created when we bring this quality into conversation can yield unexpected value for our clients and inspire them to take action. My belief is that clients will remember an agent who partners with them over one who sets out to *impress* and *convince*. In an industry where we can sometimes feel commoditized—in other words, consumers viewing us as being all the same—isn't it as important as ever to stand out from your competitors, but in a way that is less about *presenting* and *telling* and more about *asking* and *collaborating*?

Let's use the framework!

As I see it, the very act of coaching a client can be rendered powerless without the right ingredients (also known as "framework") being present.

"Shall we just paint over the old wallpaper?" A question asked, an action taken in many old English homes over the years, with unfortunate results complementing the absence of forethought or commitment to doing it right.

In conversational terms, how can we best equip ourselves toward "doing it right"?

What does this even mean? Who measures whether something is right or wrong? When a client can accept and acknowledge some accountability and agrees to manage it through specific actions, we have some great potential toward achieving results. For example, if a home seller insists on listing their home way above the comparable market value and refuses to listen to logic and remain without any accountability to price, then it is very difficult to maximize potential for them.

"Motivation" is an over-used word, especially in real estate circles, yet is a crucial factor in helping determine desire, commitment, and readiness for change. Through the nuances of coaching style, posture, concentration, and listening without judgment or the dispensing of instant-fix solutions, using this person-based lens allows for the establishment of an extraordinarily powerful coaching platform.

Case in point: don't fall into the self-imposed trap of talking about price all the time. If all a home seller hears from you is: "You're overpriced. If you want to sell, you need to reduce your price. Are you willing to?" then it becomes exclusively a price-based decision framed by a solution-based question. If, instead, the agent engages the client and moves down into P1 and P2 by asking great questions around the impacts on their lifestyle should their home remain unsold, then it becomes person-based and more meaningful for the client. I bet many in our industry have these conversations that feature price as the dominant topic, especially in a falling market, as opposed to looking at the challenge through a different lens. **Then, when the client says no, they are unable to shift the client's thinking and inspire adjustment.**

I find the simple term "unpacking" very resonant— it helps a client visually imagine their challenge and then deconstruct pieces of it before putting the picture back together in a different way. The concept of "back-swing" is another key to a client-centred approach in conversation. It refers to how we are often best served by looking back first and analyzing who and where we are, in order to take a really positive and meaningful step forward.

The person-based and solution-based approaches, when brought together as suggested by our Elevator, is remarkably beneficial to our clients. One complements the other very effectively. The opportunity for professional growth arises from working out the transition between coaching and mentoring, and knowing when to transition to the solutions phase of conversation. Here's my recommendation: stay committed to having an authentic, meaningful, and spontaneous conversation rather than a pre-planned one, and check in on occasion with your client—"How are we doing so far?" It is great partnership language to use and you'll likely sense a great time to make that transition.

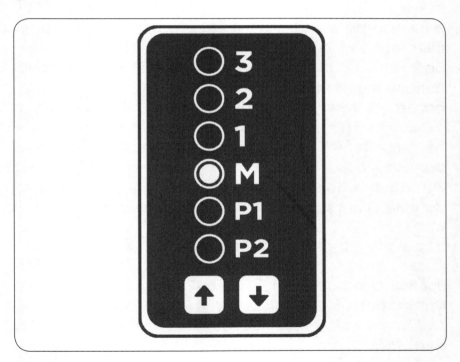

So, going back to the elevator panel, let's be clear on our understanding of where these two concepts of solution-based and person-based interactions reside. As we have discovered earlier, level 3 can be considered the culmination of all the work you and your client have fulfilled together. Levels 1 and 2 represent the early and mid-stages of reaching level 3 successfully. M is our starting point, the "what would you like to get out of our conversation?" beginning that we can absolutely choose to take. We move to P1 as we start to dig into what lies behind the objective and then down into P2 as we really help our clients work through all of their challenges. So, below M we have the person-based phase and above M is our solution-based phase. It is of course highly likely that you will dip down below M while in the solutions part of conversation, and that is just fine.

The key, in my opinion, is not just to stay above M, unless, for example, the client specifically instructs you that they don't wish to answer any questions. Even then, my natural curiosity would likely want to carefully and appropriately challenge that.

Think about times in your career when a potential client has been purposefully abrupt with you. On those occasions, was there a hidden underlying reason? It may be that they have already selected an agent to work with or feel they are being forced by a family member to choose a friend to list their property.

This spells opportunity. By being the agent who is able to decipher and bring into the open the pre-existing challenge for that potential client, it will differentiate you. It should go without saying that you are always respectful when engaging in client conversations, and isn't it fair to expect the same? As you build and refine these skills, what seems daunting today will become easier over time. In fact, at the end of one of my courses, an agent said to me, "It is harder now not to have the tough conversations." Let your intuition be your guide.

As someone else once said to me, "If you want to play a musical instrument, there is a formula. Chords need to be learned within a structure or framework that governs that world of music. Once you have mastered these, the magic can flow freely."

Coaching is much the same, and, as we come towards the next sections of the book that delve into perspectives on conversations and presentations, and how to master "the Conversational Contract," you'll start to better understand and take on board the value and power of some of the ICF Core Competencies, and you will better understand the structure and framework that mirrors for conversation what happens for music.

Are you open to a paradigm shift?

When we have a genuine yearning to learn from others and an ever-present curiosity about how we might be able to do things a little better, we tend to feel a sense of inspiration and openness. Most of us appreciate it when someone is willing to share their thoughts and ideas in any walk of life, as contrasted with someone who is all closed up and unwilling to share. The generosity of spirit I have witnessed from many other wonderful coaches and real estate people inspired me to bring this material together in a way that promotes key concepts in an easy-to-understand format, which may then be implemented using simple language and recommendations.

Taking into account the aforementioned ICF definition of coaching, what if we are able to design our own sales process so that it embodies the spirit and meaning of this definition? Out of the window, by necessity, fly the traditional sales techniques and closing procedures. In comes a meaningful engagement that serves to parallel the intention of a willing seller making a sale and a willing buyer making a buying decision.

Merriam-Webster defines a paradigm shift as "an important change that happens when the usual way of thinking about or doing something is replaced by a new and different way."

Now, on one hand, I am not asking you to throw the baby out with the bathwater and give up how you currently run your business. On the other hand, I am asking you to find those golden nuggets, those wonderful a-ha moments when something you read makes you think "wow, I never thought of that; I can really implement that!" and then go do it—take a stab at shifting your own paradigm.

What do you believe about preparation and change?

Looking down at the Mount Everest South Base Camp from 18,500 feet is startlingly powerful: the scale and beauty of the Himalayas engulfing you; snow swirling around the towering peak in the distance; the staggering size and starkness of the rock face above the tiny tents perched precariously by the Khumbu Icefall, the inhabitants of which are desperately hoping to scale the remaining 10,529 feet to the top of the world, despite ambient oxygen levels around 50 percent of those at sea level, and lower as one ascends. Back in 1987, my dream had been reached through the hard trek to base camp. For others, the dream was just beginning. This is not a place for the incompetent, but for the consciously competent.

Every expedition was outfitted with the best gear, supplies, and expertise, along with a common sense of purpose and a clear goal. Every member was equipped with specific personal skills to play their part, things like sheer determination, massive stamina, commitment to a dream, or physical ability. Each expedition member would know in advance the horrors that they would have to suffer through in the "death zone" above 26,000 feet on the way to the summit. Without enormous inner mental strength, they would never prevail.

It took a lot of commitment to reach that base camp. That was as far as I wanted to go. It was magnificent, and, from my perspective, a big milestone achieved. It took vastly more mental resources and preparation for those who had a much higher objective—and all respect to them.

Focusing back in on your real estate career, how can you prepare for a higher objective, in the sense of being the very best equipped real estate agent you can be? I believe that people must have the desire inside them to change or achieve their goals. Like thousands of others, I have found that running marathons has the same key factors: mental strength and physical preparedness. You can't typically just tell someone to go and run 42 km. The barrier—or in this case, wall—is typically reached at around 35 km. Your body is screaming for a break, but your mind is able to stay in control as long as inner desire is there. So, we understand that preparation is dramatically important, and with that a goal is possible.

Within the real estate business, if agents are prepared by visualizing a goal and can be coached to develop their own capacity to achieve it, they are actually powered

through a person-based approach and that which lies within them.

We are in an industry that is very focused on solutions. The questions that new agents are taught to ask are nearly all solution-based. It's not that they are bad questions; in fact, they are generally all pretty good ones. The challenge is that the agents are eager to move conversations forward (because it seems easier than going deep), and they believe that through some basic engagement they can win over a potential client and move forward together. Sometimes that happens. However, so many journeys that start positively with clients end without success, which leads to mutual frustration and no compensation for time and effort. Who needs that? Neither client nor the agent.

We carry around so much fear with us, often without pausing to consider the impact that it has on both ourselves and our clients—fear not only based on the legal and contractual requirements that we assume with a real estate license, but fear of failing, fear of being unable to answer questions, fear of trying to think and act outside of how agents typically compete. And then we wonder why some consumers look at agents as interchangeable commodities! We like to think we all do things differently, but take a step back for a moment and consider this question: what is truly different in how you work versus the other licensees in your market?

Summary of core principles and self-reflection
Our Learning objectives were to understand:
- **How to use the Elevator Ride to connect with your clients**

- **The eleven Core Competencies of the International Coach Federation**
- **How ICF defines the responsibilities of a coach**
- **What coaching actually is (and is *not*)**
- **The importance of curiosity**
- **The relevance of reframing your conversations and making a conscious shift in how you approach them**

Now is an opportunity to reflect on how the Elevator Ride imagery can apply in the work you do. How can using it help you to reframe and refine the methods you use to interact with your clients?

As you contemplate this, here are some good questions to ask yourself as good reference points:

Operational mode:
What type of questions do you typically ask? When serving your clients, do you tend to ask mainly solution-based questions?

Have you been trying to engage clients using an elevator pitch, or are you open to taking the Elevator Ride with them?

Which floor are you on? Do you spend enough time below the main floor, down there in P1 and P2?

Can you see how the ICF Core Competency framework helps guide you to structure a high-value conversation?

How do the four responsibilities of a coach, as defined by ICF, apply in the work you do? Can you see a relevance in each of them?

Conversational mode:
Do your typical business interactions focus primarily on providing solutions or on the other person/people?

What adjustments can you make to how you engage in conversation, bearing in mind the simplicity and phase distinctions offered through the Elevator Ride?

What's behind the scenes for you?
Have you lost some of your curiosity? How curious are you, compared to when you were a child?

Do you consider yourself to be naturally curious?

Are you surprised at what coaching actually is?

Are you also surprised to learn what it is not?

How open are you to making a paradigm shift?

How far do you want to go in being the most effective agent you can be? What do you need to prepare and change?

What action steps within your control are required to stimulate powerful conversations and enact meaningful change and empowered client decisions?

Section 3

Our Role, Our Value, and How We Compete

Understanding the fullness of our role can be challenging, especially in the context of using similar sets of presentation tools to try to out-compete each other.

This section's learning objectives are to understand
- **Our role and the basis upon which we compete**
- **How we can empower ourselves with our own system**
- **Value and how that relates to solutions**
- **The effect of assumptions, prescriptions, and pronouncements**

What is our role?

I remember years ago attending an annual sales rally and hearing the keynote speaker start by asking one simple question: "Who here is in sales?" The room comprised some 250 attendees and a mix of real estate sales professionals, property managers, and staff. By our own interpretation of what our work roles were, only some of those directly involved as "sales professionals" raised their hands—playing straight into the speaker's hands. Why? Because, as he pointed out in his next sentence, we are *all* in sales, no matter what our function might be.

That message has stayed with me ever since. Indeed, we are all in sales, from the moment we get up to the point we end our day. Think how many conversational interactions we have on a daily basis. Think about the importance of attitude and approach with these interactions, which have an enormous impact on the outcome and how people interact with us.

That term "sales professional" is an interesting one. As you fill in an order for business cards, for example, how many of you have paused to contemplate exactly what job title you should put beneath your name? In real estate sales, depending on the country you practice in and the requirements of your own licensing authority, options may include "sales associate", "Realtor®", "REALTOR®", "consultant", "advisor", "estate agent" or "real estate agent" amongst others. Isn't it interesting how, despite the fact that we all share what's essentially the same sales license, we have differing opinions about what we call the *actual role* we play?

Consider for a moment a brand-new agent struggling to make that decision and asking the advice of others. There they are, running-gear on, poised right at the starting line of their exciting new career ... and there's a lack of crystal clarity! Therein lies one of the big challenges that agents face in our industry: what should be listed out as our job description and the actual functions that we should be performing on a daily basis? Sure, there are lots of good resources available from companies and experts who believe they have the best system out there for being successful, and many of these systems have some wonderful components to them and are extremely helpful. However, here's how I see the problem: think about how we are all *told* we should eat and drink healthily and in moderation, exercise regularly, eliminate stress, and get plenty of sleep. Most of us have these good intentions yet find it very difficult to execute them all on a consistent basis. If someone *tells* us we should do these things, do we really take ownership for those actions? We might for a period of time, then fall back on our typical routines.

Same thing with systems. Over the years, I have seen so many agents searching outside of themselves for the perfect system. It is a word that we tend to place synonymously with agent success: "He has a great system; I wish I had one!" These system-driven agents have typically developed a strategic business plan that focuses on specific and consistent actions which align with their own purpose and objectives and deliver tangible, defined value for their clients. To the casual licensed observer, they appear highly organized, driven, impressive—yet somehow much different from them. Why?

Let's just park that thought for a moment and think about how incredibly rewarding a career in real estate sales can be. Tremendous professional satisfaction can be gained through playing a key role in enriching your clients' lives and achieving their real estate goals. This enables you as an agent to live a fruitful and rewarding existence. This career path attracts new agents every year from all walks of life—past engineers, nurses, or teachers, some fresh out of university, all sharing a desire to run their own businesses under the umbrella of a brokerage. They start out full of optimism, ideas, energy, and enthusiasm, and they share the belief that they will succeed and be able to find enough clients to build and sustain that business.

Yet, the rate of attrition in our industry remains very high. What is behind that?

Back to systems. While some agents simply decide it is not the career for them, my personal belief is that three major factors come into play for the many who quit. Firstly, they cannot find enough clients to serve. Secondly, they run out of the financial resources required to support both their businesses and personal circumstances. Thirdly, they fundamentally never truly work out their role, its potential, and how to actively support it on a daily basis. This third one is what intrigues me the most. How do we support our role?

I believe that many agents are working with a deficit mindset gnawing away at them because they feel they could be doing so much better. Some are unable to see themselves being as successful as others and truly carry around a belief that they are somehow deficient. This then becomes magnified when they tell you they don't have a system. Thinking back for a moment, I remember asking a group of about a dozen agents, "Who here has a system for their business?" A few hands slowly rose. I could sense how this topic immediately hit a nerve. I knew then I was on to something, and as I probed a little further with that group, I asked those who said that they had no system how they actually felt, and the words offered up included "regret," "fear," intimidated," and "a long way to go."

How enlightening was that? I also go back to another conversation with an agent about systems. I had said to him, "I see too many agents who say they have no system and are looking outside for the magic one they can copy into their own businesses. My personal belief is that everyone has a system, no matter how small. It just needs developing. Once the foundations are in place, they can add an element or two from outside."

He said to me, "You just nailed that right on the head. You can't just take someone else's system model and make it your own, that doesn't work. But you can put your own spin on someone else's proven concepts."

That is a reality of our industry: while a small percentage of agents are able to adopt other's systems, the vast majority are just not wired that way. And I don't see that as such a problem! In fact, this book is structured to help you understand your role and to enable you to develop and refine your own system. To help with that, what *is* a system? To me, there are two key parts to it; first, it is identifying all of your client-generating groups and then coming up with a methodology for developing and maintaining contact with them on a frequent basis. New business comes either from people you know and have developed trust with, or from people you do not know, which is the initial generation of "leads." Second, it is how we approach our contacts in actual conversation that forms a key part of the system. That second part is what the competencies in this book aim to support, and here's a simple systems map that aims to help you see the main pieces of your system:

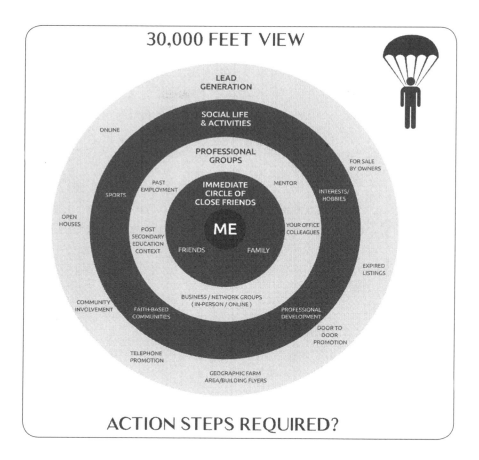

As you can see, this enables an agent to have a simple look at their business from a Himalayan 30,000 feet—in essence, stepping back and seeing a fuller picture. With you in the centre, you are invited to identify and build out the people and the group names to see where you have influence—and what elements you actually have in your system.

Use a blank version to map out your networks, and ask yourself if you are doing the best job possible in connecting with everyone. Is there an area to focus in on specifically? Who do you need to have conversations with? What action steps can you identify?

Let's not forget that the essence of the role of the real estate sales professional is entrepreneurial and includes many different facets of running a business. There are revenues and expenses, there is marketing and bookkeeping, there is subject matter and contractual expertise ... and then there is one of the biggest determinants of career success or failure: the depth and quality of interpersonal skills.

So, what if you consider your role as being that of a coach? What if we come from a mindset of servitude? Instead of *telling* and *presenting*, you *ask* and *engage*. Nice and simple. Modern and valuable. Would you like to develop the "how to"? Read on ...

How do we choose to compete?

"I have a listing presentation next week" is industry-speak about an upcoming conversation between a potential seller and a real estate agent. Those words hardly sound like a spontaneous and collaborative engagement that aims to fundamentally help a potential client think through what they want to achieve and be listened to and understood, do they? They sound like an agent justifying why they should be the one chosen for the listing.

Adjusting our perspective of an appointment can be invaluable. Let's contemplate for a second some factors involved in a potential seller choosing their listing agent out of perhaps three they have invited round to look at their home.

Some of the traditional sales training teaches agents how to win the listing. You're in competition. You may or may not have a pre-existing relationship or have been referred from someone mutually known, so you decide you have to pull out all the stops to stand out with a great marketing plan, clever branding, awesome photos, pre-scripted closing questions, and so on. For many agents, the conversation devolves into a presentation because they are pinning their hopes on their plan and marketing collateral being more appealing than that of the competition. They feel adept at handling any objections that might come up around pricing, fees charged, holding open houses or not, etcetera. It becomes a traditional "*present* and *tell*" conversation as opposed to one which focuses in on the client and actually deeply engages them.

Here's what I believe: if you focus on winning the listing, then you are likely sounding and showing up just like the other two agents you are competing with.

Price is price, marketing is marketing, there cannot really be an enormous differentiation between them. Let the other agents focus on that. I invite you to instead focus on winning the client and earning the listing. There's a subtle but huge difference there. By winning over the client, you're likely increasing your chances of being awarded the listing. By this, I mean you build a positive level of trust and understanding and create a comfortable and safe space to engage in conversation in a deeper and meaningful way for your potential client, authentically and spontaneously. You are just as prepared as any other agent, and while your presentation package is probably even more impressive than those of your competitors, it is there mainly as visual support to your verbal and physical presence with the client.

Do you put yourself in your client's shoes, or do you just comfortably stay in your own? Let that one sink in for a moment …

Our industry remains full of words like "presentations," "scripts," and "dialogues," a here's-what-you-say and here's-how-you-handle-objections kind of approach that I believe is becoming anachronistic. What's your take on that?

On what actual basis do you compete?

In November 2018, I became president of the Vancouver chapter of the International Coach Federation (ICF) at our annual general meeting. I remember that evening with fondness, as we had a great guest speaker, coach and author Alexia Vernon, share her insights. As I listened to her stories, I reframed them into my world of real estate and the types of conversations my colleagues and I have. Amongst Alexia's many valuable insights, what really landed with me that evening was identifying how we compete and the very basis of competition.

In the highly competitive real estate industry, how do you compete? Stop and think about that for a moment—how do you actually compete as a real estate agent? On what basis? We start out with our own preconceptions and look outside of ourselves to find out how others compete. We see many company brands, then we notice a multitude of personal brands, and so we start to develop our own that we feel might compete with those. We want to be noticed, we strive to position ourselves to be in the running for consumers when they require real estate services and hope that our messaging resonates with them.

But, as I heard from the longest serving and highest producing agent in the room share with his group in answer to that question, "Many in our industry seem primarily focused on trying to out-compete and out-market each other." Some of the most prolific personal brands are everywhere—the back of buses, bus benches ... it seems that they're all over the place. For some, this is what they excel at and it enables them to enjoy highly successful careers as the consummate marketers they are. But ask yourself: do you really *want* to, or *can* you, take part in the personal marketing competition? Do you have the deep financial resources or know-how? More importantly, is that how you want to drive your business into the future?

Traditional training includes an obsession with "how to present." Imagine a home seller inviting three agents round who each believe they have the very best presentation. Instead of arriving full of genuine curiosity and commitment to having a thought-provoking and high-value conversation that delves into the things that influence a prospective client's goals and objectives, they show up ready to present and *tell* why they are the best agent to list the home. After all, their package is awesome, and their approach is highly persuasive. It has landed other listings, so why not rinse and repeat? Let's call this the Presentation Game. Is this the basis upon which you want to compete in future?

What if we commit to driving our businesses from the inside out, whereby we strive to engage clients through collaboration rather than presentation? Instead of playing a leading role, we play a guiding role—in essence walking alongside our clients as we help them discover and identify motivations, fears, hopes, and aspirations. Powerful stuff indeed.

How can you bring a fresh perspective to a familiar topic? If the familiar topic is a listing presentation, how can we refresh that? We can make it look more beautiful and more comprehensive, and that's all good and of value. **But what if the true refreshment is in the *how* of engagement, and being engaged in spontaneous, not pre-planned conversation?**

So, if we agree that having a rich and attractive presentation package is still vitally important, and that engaging in a coaching conversation is of greater value as a modern option than just presenting, then how can we create a spontaneous presentation? Interesting thought, eh?

The beauty of spontaneous presentation is that it provides a gateway for satiating the urge to *present* by incorporating all your valuable presentation materials into the conversation in an authentic, high-value way. Instead of launching into your presentation, you take verbal cues that develop through the authentic, unrushed conversation as a natural entry into how something in your package fulfills a specific need.

I do not expect that we take presentation out of the industry—not at all. Instead, my aim is to challenge the very essence of what constitutes an effective interaction with a prospective buyer or seller. We can still incorporate high-value materials and share them in a meaningful and appropriate way that aligns with the client-driven dialogue rather than forcing it into an agent-driven direction.

The essence of this goal is to find out what exactly is important to your prospective client and then be able to demonstrate your competency with regard to that specific point. Here's a simple example. You ask:

"I am curious: what is important for you when it comes to marketing your home?"

"I just want to make sure that we maximize our exposure in the market and get as many qualified buyers to look as possible."

"Great. If I can share with you a comprehensive marketing plan that has that richness and reach, would you like to see that?"

"Sure, that would be great."

This now gives client-driven permission to share your plan.

You are free to choose the basis on which you compete. The key is to be clear about what actually inspires and empowers you, and fundamentally differentiates you.

Our perception of what our value is

These days, most consumers know roughly what their homes are worth. If providing the value of their home is your principal value, then how are you different from other agents?

Earlier in the chapter, we talked about our perceptions of what our actual role is. What about our *value*? We start out passing an examination and obtaining a license. Then we start looking for buyers and sellers we can help, while developing our promotional materials and learning all about the business from various courses and sources. Then we embrace—as one tends to do in any field—some of the industry jargon, and what happens when you actually get in front of a buyer or seller? That's when the mind goes into *presentation* mode.

I have long maintained that our value lies in three main areas: our ability to negotiate, our ability to deeply interpret market knowledge and all market influencers, and passionately and genuinely care for our clients. That last one is an enormous responsibility and our profession is well served by codes of ethics and standards that must be adhered to. What I believe happens is this: because we consider ourselves subject-matter experts to differing degrees, we feel the need to demonstrate this quickly when meeting with a buyer or seller. We are fearful that if we don't demonstrate our value quickly, they will dismiss us as an agent unworthy of helping them. That is a real issue and speaks to many factors, such as mindset and confidence, which we'll cover later. What if we refine that demonstration of value to be a client-focused conversation that aims to help the clients clearly articulate a vision for what they wish to accomplish? Doesn't that sound valuable? We really need to take a good hard look at what we each consider to be valuable for our clients.

Assumption of expectation

Let's look at it this way: you are engaged in a professional conversation with a client, the topic being right in your comfort wheelhouse and in your realm of expertise. You have been waiting for this exciting decision-making moment to come and you are eager to share your expertise and wisdom. It makes you feel good to position yourself as the knowledge resource and influencer. The assumption we make is this: this is why the client has sought me out to work with. Well, most likely it is—that expertise lies at the centre of your value proposition. But an important question is this: **how can you truly and positively impact your client by detaching from outcome and assumption?** The answer is to engage in the moment to help your client refine exactly what they feel is their best course of action and to be of service to that. This has the benefit of actually removing, for both of you, any limitation or ceiling on potential. How good does that sound? Finding out what is really behind an objective and what else is important to that person is crucial. Quick point: most agents I know already do this, but to a limited extent. Challenge your assumptions!

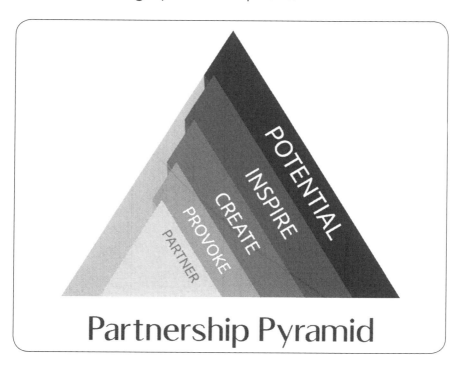

Partnership Pyramid

So, what if you release yourself from the urge to provide *your* solutions?

As humans, it is very difficult to lose weight, gain weight, eat more, eat less, work out more, work out less if someone tells us that we should. **By contrast, if someone asks us simple, thought-provoking questions that challenge us in well-intentioned ways to discover how our own motivations and actions impact our life, then our own self-generated solutions have way more chance of making sense**. Not only that, they have a much longer shelf life.

Years ago, I sat with a client who had hired me as his real estate agent/listing agent and worked through a number of offers. I recall we had three or four, and the seller was happy to allow each agent to come and present them. One stood out. The agent, a great guy, took forever to tell us why his buyer loved the home and what the emotional connection was, and he finally arrived at a price that was much lower than the eventual successful offer. Looking back, I suspect he had been given some training on how to present an offer. What was lacking was *engagement*. He was trying too hard. He dominated the discussion by *telling* instead of offering us his calm presence and engaging us in collaborative conversation. Yes, his price was much lower, but it was magnified through the one-sidedness of the dialogue.

In the extreme, a *present*-and-*tell* type of interaction can manifest itself as a disengaging barrage of words and opinions that do little to help a client make a good buying or selling decision. In modern-day communication, while you can believe that you sell your value through telling, you can actually build and deliver it valuably through *asking* and *sharing*. When we take the *telling* approach, we tend to assume command and fall in line with the *presentation* way of dialogue. If we are sitting on a see-saw, our client is somewhere up in the air. Can you remember that feeling? It's hardly one of security or togetherness.

When we *ask*, we start to engage and collaborate. We start the process of working together in a way that draws out values and beliefs and enables the ability of our client to make fully engaged decisions—which is of the most benefit to them. If we avoid *telling*, it is amazing what can happen. We dance in conversation through the ICF competencies, we take the Elevator Ride up and down a few times, work up through the Partnership Pyramid— authentically, patiently, curiously.

So, think about the concept of value and how you are showing up—back to the identification of the basis or bases on which you compete. If you would like to develop and build an inherent ability to coach your clients, then this approach has you covered. Value is central to pretty much everything in life. If we are unsure of our value heading into the future, we're not in a very good place, are we?

Why *prescribe* and *pronounce*?

The bottom line is that it is actually easier to *prescribe* a course of action to someone and *pronounce* your own opinions. We do it all the time.

An example scenario for this might be something like: "Well, here's what I'd do in your situation. I wouldn't buy the lower floor; I'd go for the top floor every time because ..."

It is certainly easier and seems to appear to be the best way to go, because we perceive that we are able to *deliver the value the client is expecting.* Right? However, in many situations, it will be less effective. Why is that?

Let's look at an analogy from the gym. It is common knowledge that gyms are brimming with people during the first few months of the year as resolutions kick into place. Yet as spring approaches and the weather gets better, those numbers dwindle as most members fail to show consistently. Have you ever noticed how often you see the same people at the gym when *you* are going regularly? It all comes down to purpose and motivation—the *why*.

Imagine a conversation with someone who says to you, "I need to start working out. I want to get fit." It is amazing how quickly most people will take a solution-based approach. This might go something like this:

"Great, sounds exciting. Do you belong to a gym?"

"No, I don't."

From here we go straight to solutions ...

"Well, I go to the Fitness Gurus, it's awesome. Why don't you come with me and I'll show you around?"

"Sure, sounds good."

A couple of months later, chances are high that they have joined but are starting to go less and less often. How could we approach this in a more meaningful way?

"Great, sounds exciting. Do you belong to a gym?"

"No, I don't."

Now a move into person-based dialogue ...

"Okay, so you want to get fit. What is driving that thought?"

"Hmm, good question. I have noticed I have less energy these days and I have a sedentary job. I actually do very little exercise, so it seems a good idea to join a gym."

"So, sounds as if you'd like to increase energy levels. What other objectives do you have?"

"I'd like to drop about five pounds, get out more, and do some fun activities."

"What kinds of things interest you?"

"I would love to go hiking and try paddle-boarding. It looks fun!"

"So ... is this really about joining a gym, or about working out an activity plan that will help you reach your objectives?"

"You're right. Actually, to be honest, the gym sounds kind of boring."

"I am curious—what would you like to get out of our conversation?"

"Hmm, good question, let me think ... I'd like to talk about what else I could do to get fitter and have fun at the same time."

"Just to be clear, you'd like us to explore different options to help you reach your goal?"

"Absolutely."

"And what specifically would you like to walk away with?"

"I would like to have two to three new outdoor activities that I decide to go and sign up for. That would be awesome."

See the difference? If we are able to *draw out* from our client instead of *telling* them, we are moving forward *together* as partners sharing a mission to accomplish what the client is looking for, and then the solutions that *they* develop through our skillful questioning have a greater chance of delivering value. As part of this collaborative process, it is imperative that we help coach our friend all the way through to identifying the activities, the action steps to reach them, and also a plan to keep them accountable to it. It is their solution, not just ours.

Perspective itself

We have a tendency to see things from our own perspective. We also tend to believe that our perspective is the right (and perhaps only) one. Picture two people in a lofted room—one is below and one is up in the loft area, leaning over. The person below takes a towel, extends an arm, and makes a clockwise circular motion with the towel. The one above asks, "So, can you share with me what you're seeing?" The person below says, "Of course, it's pretty obvious that I am waving this towel over my head in a clockwise direction." Of course, to the person above it is actually moving in the opposite direction, yet the person below cannot see it from that perspective so offers up their confident opinion based purely on their vision.

How we choose to look at things and interpret situations can be quite different when we have someone who can help us see the whole picture.

When a home seller or home buyer is fixated on a position—for example, a buyer is asking you to write an offer on a new, reasonably well-priced listing in a balanced market that is 20 percent below the asking price—it is important that we can bring into play another perspective. Here are two examples of ways to handle that:

"So, you want to lowball and offer $720,000 on this $899,000 listing? That's really low. I don't think you have any chance."

"I'd just like to try it. You never know."

"Okay, we can try!"

Versus:

"I'm hearing that you would like to offer $720,000 on this $899,000 listing when you shared with me that the closest comparable sales all point between $860,000–$875,000. Can you share with me where that $720,000 figure comes from?"

"I'd just like to try. You never know."

"What do you believe could be the reaction of the seller for offering so low?"

"Well, they can always counter me."

"Can we take a look at this from the perspective of the seller? They have listed quite reasonably at $899,000, and the lowest recent comparable sale was $865,000. If you were in their shoes, how would you react to $720,000?"

"Hmm. I guess it's very low. It's just that I want to get a deal."

"Okay, thanks for sharing that. Can you define for me what a deal would look like?"

And onwards the conversation would go, delving into the thinking of this buyer and the actual impact of making a poor decision. The more you can help your real estate clients see a larger picture, the greater the likelihood they will make better decisions. Who doesn't want a deal when they shop? But by having them define for you what a deal would look like and then engaging in a conversation about the impact of their choices, you can only increase the chance of better client-generated solutions. If not, remember—you can only do your best. We simply cannot help everyone we come across. But our work is all about giving ourselves and our clients the best possible chances for a successful negotiation.

What happens when a client asks for my opinion?

A fascinating part of the sales process is this: what happens when a client asks what *you* think they should do? This is a critical point in the process of sales. And this is perhaps the key to understanding the power of *ask* versus *tell*.

- How much should I offer?
- Which one would you choose?

- How much would you offer?
- What would you do in my situation?

The clear temptation is to switch straight back into *telling* mode. It is essential that we understand why this happens. If you step back for a second and contemplate this, what are you thinking? Are you a tad confused, maybe wondering if this isn't why consumers employ us in the first place: to provide professional opinions, advice, and analysis? Indeed, that is true. However, what happens if we are the ones providing the solutions? On one hand, that sounds like high value. On the other, the sustainable buy-in to the solutions you have offered up might be relatively weak and come with a degree of inherent risk.

An offer price is a great example that illustrates how, by providing a price suggestion, you are opening yourself up to very substantial risk. What if the client later regrets offering *your* price? What if they would have been willing to offer more than you suggest, and they lose the property in a competitive situation? A great way to limit that potential is to commit to eliciting client-generated solutions. It also increases potential to achieve better mutual results. And isn't that our objective?

Let's look at one of the client's questions above.

"How much should I offer?"

"Well, if I were you I would …" is a straight *tell*. Instead, how about:

"That's a great question. As you reflect on the comparable sales that we just looked at, what price is coming up for you?" Then, stay with the coaching and resist jumping in and pronouncing your opinion. With careful questioning around the decisions that are surfacing, you will help refine and clarify your client's thinking and increase their confidence in what has resulted. Of course, if it is a price that realistically has no chance of being accepted (for example, a weak offer in a multiple-offer scenario), then you can coach your client to see things from the receiving seller's perspective and understand what impact it will have on your buyer's objectives.

Similarly, "what would you do in my situation?" can be answered in the same fashion, authentically striving to help your client make the best decision.

Summary of core principles and self-reflection

Our Learning objectives were to understand:
- **Our role and the basis upon which we compete**
- **How we can empower ourselves with our own system**
- **Value and how that relates to solutions**
- **The effect of assumptions, prescriptions, and pronouncements**

Bearing in mind all these conversation and presentation perspectives, think about how you can apply some of these principles in the work you do. What opportunities are there if you reframe and refine your interactions with clients?

As usual, some good questions to ask yourself as good reference points:

Operational mode:
How do you see your role?

What do you believe is your value upon which you compete?

Do you want to be a solution provider or a solution generator?

Conversational mode:
Are you typically a dispenser of advice, answering most questions immediately?

Do you find you do most of the talking?

Which do you do more of, coaching your clients or providing prescriptive solutions?

Are you heavy on selling and convincing and light on authentic curiosity, listening, and understanding?

What's behind the scenes for you?
Do you need to release yourself from any assumptions, fears, and projected outcomes?

What action steps within your control are required to stimulate powerful conversations and help enact meaningful change and better empowered client decisions?

Are you on the way to building deeper, effective working relationships with your clients?

Section 4

Conversation and Presentation Perspectives

Real estate sales as a career has traditionally been very presentation-driven. Stop for a moment and consider: how can your clients benefit if you adjust your approach?

Learning objectives are to understand:
- **The power of *collaborating* versus *telling***
- **The essence of coaching as a process**
- **How to reframe our thinking on presentations**
- **The difference between using predetermined scripts and spontaneous conversation**
- **How to simply define what the conversation is about**

Harnessing the power of collaboration to level the playing field

What if we look at the actual sales process through a different lens than we are used to, and strive to share a level playing field with our clients? That old saying "there is no 'i' in team" speaks to the difference in teamwork versus individual dominance—an agent's consistent operating standard and procedure should aim to build a powerful collaboration between herself and the client, rather than one where objections are adversarially handled through a "you can throw any objection at me and I'll win" kind of mentality.

How could that key shift in dynamic impact the conversation?

One of the reflection questions at the end of the last section was: "Do you find you do most of the talking?" A good way to gauge how genuinely collaborative you are is to reflect on the amount of talking that goes on when you are with a client or prospective client, and in particular who is doing the majority of it. When we do most of the talking, we are essentially in "tell mode." We take a question as being the perfect cue to impart our knowledge. When you commit to engaging through collaboration, you cannot just sit there and *tell*. You have to *ask*, otherwise there is no real collaboration.

There is also a collaborative approach to those traditional objections that occur in real estate sales. For example, consider a conversation where your client is listing their property with you and there is a lively discussion around the actual list price. Ultimately, the client should make the pricing decision based on as clear a picture as possible of both their choice of options (for example, right around or lower or higher than the expected price) and the potential impact for each. Let's say a comparable market analysis shows that the worth of the home is in the range of $700,000–$725,000 and that a sensible asking price that suits the current market conditions is $729,000–$739,000. The homeowner expresses that they would like to start out at $850,000, as they feel their home is quite special and they are in no hurry.

The agent is now facing a very common challenge: should I just take the listing as stipulated by the client? Should I argue down the list price? Imagine if the conversation goes south and starts to become disengaging and judgemental, unfriendly and combative? What impact could that have, both now and in future conversation?

"Well, that's way too high! We'll never sell your home!"

In an engaging conversation, we have a choice between challenging back as partners rather than as adversaries.

"So, I'm hearing from you that your preferred pricing strategy is to start high. I am curious, which of the comparables is your $850,000 based on?"

"Well, I have no hurry ... and my home is better than all the others."

"Okay, I understand how much you value your home. What if we take a look from a buyer's perspective, and see what they can buy between $700,000 and $850,000?"

It sets up a collaboration that engages rather than one which creates adversity.

To be crystal clear, let's take a step back and deal with the elephant in the room right now: what to do if you can't talk them down and they insist on that price? In fact, what if they say they will not sell for less?

As any experienced agent worth their salt will share, you cannot hope to work with every client you meet. Agents meet clients whom they cannot work effectively with quite often. And guess what? The same applies the other

way around—clients meet agents who are unsuited to working with them.

When you know what your values are, it becomes easier to ascertain who you can actually work with. As you learn how to partner with them, this picture will become increasingly clear for you.

A good way to think about this is considering how agents show up in negotiating an offer. According to the Real Estate Negotiation Institute, there are three main types of negotiators involved in real estate transactions: competitive, collaborative, and compliant. The institute lists out the traits of each and the effect each one has in the way they show up. In essence, *competitive* wants to win, *compliant* doesn't want to rock the boat and *collaborative* wants to help create a win for both parties, together with the cooperating agent. I believe most of us would welcome a negotiation with the collaborator, wouldn't we? In a real estate negotiation, it levels the playing field when we share a commitment to a genuine willingness and desire to bring both parties to an agreement and negotiate the various terms and conditions in good faith and spirit.

In another sense, a listing opportunity and collaboration can be a great equalizer. Imagine a listing appointment where a newer agent is competing with the area expert. The latter has the downhill slope in front of them, believing that they can use their experience to lead the whole conversation, present in exactly the way they want to, tell the potential client everything about why working with them is the best solution, and, in their experienced estimation, win the listing. By contrast, the newer agent is looking uphill, perhaps daunted by hearing that the potential client has the area expert in and wondering what they can say to compete, dreading hearing questions like: "So, how many homes have you sold in this neighbourhood?" or "How much experience do you have?"

How can that newer agent level the playing field? Through the wonderful tool of collaboration and adherence to a conversational framework based on curiosity (*asking*) and the principles used by professional coaches.

To be clear, I am not saying that any new agent can beat out the area expert every time. In appreciation of those experts who have worked tirelessly to build their businesses, what I am suggesting is that there are potential clients ahead whose business you will find harder to attract if your operational standards and procedures involve traditional sales techniques. I believe this is because the kind of communication that is heavy on selling and convincing and light on authentic curiosity, listening, and understanding will become less and less popular in general with consumers of all types, not just those in the real estate market.

Reflecting on typical coaching

I have so much respect for the work of professional managing brokers. They carry huge responsibility on their shoulders and are normally a rock for their agents. Those I have worked alongside for years are among the absolute best in the business. Their advice is constantly being sought and they play a role that is seen as vital to their agents.

Interestingly, as with the roles we all play, theirs is one which can be refreshed through the adoption of these coaching principles. Here's a simple example (for clarity, it does not suggest that all managing brokers take this approach):

A struggling real estate agent has a meeting set with his manager. Nine months into the year and with only two sales to his name, they both know that something has to change. The agent sits down and explains how he is really struggling this year and mentions that he is hoping the manager can offer some ideas on kickstarting his business. After some basic questions, the manager offers up activities the agent can do which will help him, listing them off and explaining how to perform them. The agent eagerly writes the advice down—he can't get the ideas down quickly enough—and then thanks his manager with a definitive thumbs-up for all the great suggestions before heading home. They are going to go door-knocking three mornings a week, they are going to try committing to making twenty phone calls to complete strangers each day for the next month, they are going to have coffee meetings with one person they know each day.

What happens when they reach home, open the door, and put their bag down? What happens when we go to those sales conferences that share idea after idea? We get all pumped up and excited to the point that we just can't wait to start implementing them all. Yet, a week later, we wonder where that feeling and rush of excitement has gone and most of the valuable ideas have become dim and distant, compounding the problem that we had in the first place: few sales and no proactive activity happening.

Why is this? Why does the traditional approach of sharing ideas and mentoring like this have limited chances of success with most agents? How could that manager have a much more valuable conversation with the agent? The crux lies in the first part: "... after some basic questions."

An accredited coach does not typically provide advice or dispense solutions. They listen, they ask deep questions, they challenge thinking, they seek to help the agent understand what has been holding them back from taking proactive action for those nine months. They drill down into the *why* (our P1 and P2), they look to inspire and—above all—to partner with the agent in the dialogue.

As a simple illustration, the manager's basic questions with his agent might flow like this:

"Thanks for coming in, Bob. How are you?"

"Fine thanks, and thank you for taking the time to help me."

"My pleasure. I always enjoy helping you. So, what's going on?"

"Not much—and that's the problem. I have two sales and the year is three-quarters over. I just don't know what I should do to get going again. If I can't pick things up I might have to find another job."

"Well, we don't want that to happen, do we. Will it be helpful if I give you three business-generating ideas to kickstart things?"

"Sure, that sounds great!"

And out come the suggested solutions. A coach's questions might flow more like this:

"Hi Bob, how are you today?"

"Fine thanks, and thank you for taking the time to help me."

"My pleasure. So, what's on your mind?"

"Well, to be honest, I am not doing well at all with my business. I only have two sales this year and I just don't know what I should do to get going again. If I can't pick things up I might have to find another job."

"So, I am sensing a bit of a struggle going on with your business. What's behind that?"

"I feel like I am dead in the water. I am not sure if I should just quit and find another job. Is it even the right business for me? I did really well last year, but this year the market is so different and I just can't get going."

"What I am hearing is that you *have* done well before, and now that it is not so positive, you are even wondering if it's the right business for you. So, what would you like to get out of our conversation today?"

"Good question. Am I in the right job? Is it possible for me to be successful again?"

And so begins a deep and collaborative conversation that focuses in on the person rather than on providing prescriptive solutions. Can you see the difference in approach? We are coaching the person rather than the problem. The manager thought his agent would appreciate his solid ideas; after all, he did ask if they would be helpful, so he felt he did a good job in delivering those solutions. But, essentially, it might be wide of the mark. It is highly unlikely that a struggling agent will be able to successfully implement those types of solutions. Here are three simple reasons why:

- He did not generate the solutions themselves, so he has no ownership of them
- The specific actions would need to be designed and owned by him, step by step, and an accountability plan put in place
- The "why" behind actually performing those actions would need to be crystal clear

The essence of this illustration is to open up and explore a conversation and not just go with the first thing that comes out. The manager actually delivered on the request for ideas—and delivered well. However, by shifting from a solution-providing approach he could have delivered a far more meaningful experience for his agent and it would be of longer-term value. We cannot take actions unless we are ready in ourselves to do so. You cannot tell someone it is a good idea to run a marathon; you and they are better served if they come to that conclusion by themselves.

Take a quick look again at that first sentence of this section: "A struggling real estate agent has a meeting set with his manager. Nine months into the year and with only two sales to his name, they both know that something has to change." The key is how you interpret the last four words: "something has to change." I don't believe that solutions alone are change-enabling for the majority of people.

It brings back to mind a simple chart I first saw during a class at the University of British Columbia that resonated very strongly with me. Comprised of three columns, it asked us to consider the difference between coaching, counselling, and mentoring. I quickly realized that much of what I have witnessed and been a part of over the years in my management roles has been, fundamentally, mentorship in action. It is far easier to engage with someone and offer up proactive ideas and suggestions (*command, present, tell*) rather than to go in the other direction and spend quality time helping them look within themselves (*ask, engage, collaborate*). Far easier, yet in most cases less effective. That was an *a-ha* moment for me.

Think of an iceberg—often a magnificent and enormous mass of frozen water floating along that we can see clearly ... above the waterline. But what lingers beneath? A much, much larger mountain of ice. It is only when we are able to discover the vastness of that lower mass that we can better understand the whole. Indeed, it is below the personal waterline where understanding motivations, wants, and needs really happens, yet, in most sales conversations, we rarely allow ourselves as agents or salespeople to get wet.

So, before we get more into it, let's clearly understand that mentorship generally involves *telling* and *showing* people what and how to do something, and counselling in very simple terms involves giving advice, opinions, or instructions to someone, but on a different level than coaching. It is important to make a clear distinction and to be able to understand the differences. It is not a case of which is better than the other; in fact, they all have their place. However, the point here is that so much coaching is very directive ("here's how to ...") rather than non-directive (draw out from within). If you *engage* and *draw out* instead of *tell* and *command*, it is amazing what a difference you can make.

Coaching has moved from being curative and corrective and steeped in a language of deficiency to being a language of exploration, inspiration, possibility, and creation. If you open yourself to thinking differently, then you will find yourself enjoying deeper person-centred conversations and increased engagement.

But—hang on a minute—don't we call ourselves a real estate advisor or consultant?

Absolutely, and that does not need to change. It is imperative for us to understand that our advisory and consultancy capacities do not go away; we are highly valued for those very reasons, and rightly so. Our clients want our advice and our consultancy. The key here is the process by which we provide it. What can go away is the urgency with which we tend to *tell* and *present*, even without realizing it. Someone asks a question, we answer it; they ask another, we answer it. What happens when we ask some questions back and then provide space for our clients to consider and reflect? Try it!

Do we remain interpreters of market information? Absolutely. Strong negotiators? Absolutely. Maybe we even offer concierge-type services to our clients, become a resource to them for all things real estate related. All of those qualities and requirements expected of us as licensed entities remain; the fantastic opportunity that presents itself lies in the framework within which we choose to communicate, even in these arenas. Here are a couple of simple illustrations to bring home clarity:

Buyer to agent: "I am thinking about buying my first home, but I am not sure if it's a good time or not, as a friend of mine said the market might go down later this year. What do you think I should do?"

Common type of question, common scenario. Many agents would go straight into *command, present,* and *tell* mode—aligning their value to a predisposed assumption that they need to provide answers and professional opinions.

"Well, lots of people have opinions and it's hard to say where the market may or may not be going, but it's always good to get into real estate sales rather than rentals. What are you looking for?"

We tend to move very quickly towards solutions without even realizing it. Perhaps there's a better way? How about this:

"Well Jane, doesn't that sound exciting—buying your first home! Is there something that has happened in your life that enables you to jump into the market?"

"Yes, actually, I am fortunate that my parents are able to give me $100,000 as a downpayment and I've also got a decent career started."

"Thank you for sharing that, as it helps me to understand your motivations. Now, you mentioned someone suggested to you that the market may go down later in the year—can we park that for a second? [Move your hands to the side to illustrate that parking.] I am curious, are you hoping to buy and then try to sell quickly for a profit, or is your hope to put down some roots, paint the walls, perhaps lay some hardwood flooring, and make it a real home for some years?"

"Oh, definitely the latter. I can't wait to have my very own place!"

"How are you feeling when you think about that?"

"You know, I am excited! I just hope I can get in before the prices rise further ..."

"Of course. We'll work as well as we can together to make that happen. Let's bring the market question back in now, shall we? [Move your hands back in from the side.] Based on your longer-term vision, how important is it to you whether the market goes up, down, or stays the same in the short term?"

"Hmm, now I think about that, I guess buying the right place as soon as I can makes sense. I am sick of paying that rent and it'll feel great to be paying down my own mortgage and be free in my own place."

In this simplest of illustrations, the agent asked the client to open up and explore, rather than *telling* her opinion. Agent answers such as "Well, if I were you …" or "I think the market will …" are less effective, as they are our own isolated opinions instead of what clients may come up with themselves.

Ownership of solutions is important—the more your client owns their solutions, the better the chance of you working well together. If their own solutions are not particularly workable, then challenge back—as a partner—to help them see what you can see.

To really bring home this message, imagine for a moment that natural gas prices go sky-high. Homeowners are now facing substantial bills just to heat their homes. So, an enterprising solar heating entrepreneur thinks *Great, here's my opportunity* and proceeds to mail out to a large area of homes the following message:

> Now that natural gas prices are so high, you should make the switch to solar power! Call me to arrange an appointment.

This approach involves pure *command* and *tell*, which is hardly engaging. How could it sound better?

With natural gas prices being so high today, have you thought about an alternative way to heat your home? Would you like to find out how easy it is to switch to solar power and how it compares to natural gas?

Coaching enhances authenticity of communication and provides a valuable interactive mechanism.

The coexistence of conversation and presentation

We are obsessed with presentations, absolutely obsessed with them in the real estate sales field. On one hand, this is a good thing and there is lots of value to be shared. But on the other, it is one of the root causes of blocking valuable and authentic connection with a potential client.

Why is it this way? Well, the good of presentations is that they are a valuable way to convey knowledge and how it is you interpret that knowledge, and a great way to explain your differences in marketing, expertise, and so on. It is important to add a visual component to these types of meetings.

To be clear, I do believe that a typical interaction with a potential seller or buyer should in most cases compose a portion of presentation. In fact, this is an area where many very successful agents excel in and I am not suggesting that needs to change. What might need some adjustment is *how* this wonderful material is introduced and articulated for the client. There are lots of options. A presentation can begin as the basis and mainstay of a conversation and end as a leave-behind after a thorough conversational engagement, and be useful anywhere in between.

As I see it, the challenge lies in two things: first, why do so many agents call a meeting with a prospective buyer a "buyer presentation," and one with a prospective seller a "listing presentation"? Why does the industry use these terms? See where I am going with this? It has been deeply rooted for years and years. Over time, what resources we can offer to a prospective client and the ways in which we utilize them has changed enormously, from dot-matrix printers and catalogues of homes all the way through to virtual tours, websites specific to marketing that home, drone photography, tablets—the list for showing what you can do seems almost endless in possibility, and is continually evolving.

Agents make an assumption that if they show some really cool and effective marketing tools as the mainstay of their conversation, these will become the key difference. And they might. As stated earlier, I do not denigrate any of this and actually promote all of those values and the creative minds behind them. Kudos to those agents and the creative marketing minds behind other industries who come up with fantastic marketing ideas!

Second, I believe that we *assume* a client wants a presentation. Some do, but do they all? And even if someone asks for a presentation, doesn't that leave itself open to interpretation and assumption of what that means to the client—and to us? So, how are we able to discern if a client *does* want one? Well, it is a presentation, in the sense that what is being presented is a great conversational opportunity. Cue our earlier reference to spontaneous presentation ...

Let's frame it out this way: we are meeting with a potential seller. We had a quick chat on the phone a few days before and asked several typical questions, focusing on setting up a mutually convenient appointment. The seller informed us in that call that she is having two other agents come round during the next few days to provide opinions, that she was referred to you by another client of yours, and that she would like to hear what you believe her home is worth and how you would market it. As you put the phone down, the presentation bell rings loud and clear. You tell yourself: *I have a listing presentation.* Exciting! We are humans, after all, and so we start thinking about how great it would be if we win this listing. We prepare a comparative market analysis and we work out the price range to the best of our abilities, even though we have not actually seen the inside of the house yet, and we include within our package lots of additional information, such as our profile, a marketing plan, testimonials, and awards we may have earned. We're feeling chipper—everything is ready to go, and at the agreed upon time, we reach the property and turn off the car's ignition. We turn to look at the house again. It looks familiar—we drove past yesterday as we reviewed comparable properties and familiarized ourselves as much as we could.

How are we feeling? That depends on a lot of factors, doesn't it? Experience, preparation, our mood ... there are so many pieces to this puzzle. Am I sensing some slight nerves and apprehension building as we approach the door? We might be giving ourselves a little pep talk, something like: "Okay, focus, this is it. Don't screw it up, present well, don't forget to talk about the marketing plan."

What happens then? In the kitchen or living room, we might take some time to build rapport, and, depending on how that goes, have a conversation with the client about what they want to achieve. We remember to ask all those solution-based questions, things like: "Where will you move to? When? What do you hope to buy?" We remember to touch on *why*. And then there's usually a chance to view the property and refine thoughts about price. We also remember to ask that traditional question: "What criteria do you look for in an agent?" It may be the classic one-stop listing presentation, or we may let the prospective seller know we will come back with our full pricing and marketing presentation, if that's okay, as that's what we prefer to do. As the conversation unfolds, we feel it is important to take control and let the prospective seller know what we want to talk about and *present* to them. As objections or questions come up, we answer them. Our hope is to win the listing. We might, or we might not.

Here's the question: what would happen if we allowed that presentation obsession to focus on merely having a great conversation? Instead of ramping up the pressure, it could serve to calm things down and allow perhaps the best possible thing to happen (other than successfully taking the listing with a very happy and trusting seller): for us to detach from outcome, fears, and assumptions.

- **Outcome** – We need to present to win the listing.
- **Fears** – What if we don't present well? What if we miss out on this opportunity and don't win the listing?
- **Assumptions** – Such as: "We know what we need to do here; our presentation worked like a charm last time."

By now, I believe it should go without saying that you have a high value, professional presentation package. But, as important as flour and sugar are to a cake, that detachment from presentation compulsion is an important ingredient in a client conversation. Presentation mode can actually inhibit authentic spontaneity. Think about going out with friends and how much fun and connection can be derived from spontaneous, unplanned conversation. When you exercise curiosity, don't the friends you are meeting with typically do so as well? It opens up a relaxed and trusting space to share stories, experiences, challenges, hopes, and dreams. With close friends, we can feel positive, valued, warm, cared for, grateful for each other, and any input and encouragements given or received serve to build on those feelings. We meet someone new on that evening out, a friend of a friend, and likely interact with the same vibe that has been created by the group through natural conversation that served to build connection.

What if that prospective seller is not a friend? In fact, we might not have even met them before. And we have told ourselves that we are going to *present* to them. Is it any wonder then that so many agents come out of a listing presentation unsure of how they did, perhaps feeling they could have done better had they not been nervous or better prepared? They believe their marketing plan and pricing went over okay, although the client was reluctant to commit to anything. I have heard many agents use the word "audition" for these types of meetings—*auditioning for a job*. While that is true and we are hoping to be the professional selected to serve, the audition mindset is not necessarily a helpful one, as it does tend to build self-pressure and expectation.

I remember once a newer agent sharing how his first listing presentation went. He said it was awful, as he was so nervous. He had presented to the client, and when I asked him what the client had thought their home was worth compared to his own opinion, he had no idea. As new agents, we're pretty good at ramping up the pressure on ourselves, aren't we? Actually, it's not just new agents—when you think about the *average* agent in terms of sales transaction numbers, they only have these types of listing conversations maybe, what, three to five times in a year? That is especially the case if they tend to work more with buyers.

What if, after you had set the appointment with that potential seller, you were able to refrain from using listing-presentation terminology and replaced it instead with a listing *conversation*, and committed simply to being as package-prepared as possible but arriving without fears, assumptions, or attachment to any outcome, and looking forward to having a valuable conversation? Doesn't that sound inviting? It reduces pressure and allows you to be natural. **We are well served by committing to a move away from any compulsions to control the interactions.**

It's all about connection. Did you connect on a human level with this seller?

If you're at all skeptical about this approach, I would like to recall the early days of my real estate career—without the Internet. Sure, the business processes still worked, but what if an agent in 1995 had decided to just ignore the Internet and had continued on that path until today? Change is constant and methods change with the times. Some readers might be thinking, *Well, it's all fine and dandy to say you can have a great conversation with a prospective client, but what if they don't want to?* Read on, we have you covered ...

So, are you able to train yourself to refrain from using the P-word – *presentation*? Be curious about this approach; after all, what is the worst thing that can happen?

That word: "closing"

Think of the traditional sales process in many sales industries: one person showing an interest, another often trying their best to make the sale happen through persuading, convincing, and closing. In sales environments, there have been closing rooms for years. "Let's step into the closing room, shall we?" Think about that for a moment— being invited into a room for the specific purpose of the other person obtaining your signature or agreement to purchase. Doesn't that sound rather one-sided?

Or consider the famous lines spoken in *Glengarry Glen Ross*, the 1978 movie set in a small-town real estate company, where the salesmen (played by Al Pacino, Ed Harris, and Jack Lemmon, among others) were told by Alec Baldwin's character Blake from Downtown to "A.B.C.: *Always. Be. Closing.*" While we want to come to buying decisions, doesn't this sound a tad coercive? They did assemble an outstanding cast, though ...

Of course, most skilled and appreciated salespeople wouldn't use such language. But the essence of making the sale through words spoken in a telling and convincing nature can still be there.

What happens when we revise that old saying to something like: "always be coaching," or better still, in my opinion, "always be curious"—now we're cooking with gas. More later about curiosity, which is one of the most effective and brilliant words when used authentically in so many conversational contexts, for so many reasons.

Do you believe that your clients want you to "close" them? Or would they rather you coach them through to powerful, client-generated solutions?

Scripts versus proficiencies

My focus with this book is on helping you to build some new and refined *proficiencies*, which is a term we use to collectively refer to our toolbox of coaching-based sales techniques. Take a moment to consider the difference between scripts and proficiencies. To me, scripts are language that someone mentors you to use that can either lead a conversation or handle objections, whereas proficiencies speak to underlying core competencies and an understanding and familiarity with certain fundamentals.

In some cases, scripts can be really helpful. The challenge that I have with them is that they tend to indicate that the speaker has power over the listener, and they aren't spontaneous. In her excellent work *Conversational Intelligence*, Judith E. Glaser promotes the notion of "power with others": being on the same page and sharing how each person views a topic, and she identifies different levels of this notion. If we look at how some conversations start, "How can I help you?" is an example of a "power *over* others" type of opening and sets up the conversation in a certain way. As we build our familiarity with the essence of partnership in the conversational context, we will be exploring how to bookend a conversation and move it from being a presentation-focused, closed dialogue to an engaging and collaborative open exploration of objectives and what is motivating or limiting them.

The other challenge I have is that few agents can internalize and operate using learned scripts. Moreover, scripts and closed dialogues are not natural and authentic. Is it just me, or do scripts seem to be from the era of *command, present,* and *tell*? Sure, I can see value in scripts if, for example, you are arranging an event and there is a certain consistent and detailed message that needs to be delivered. Time, location, parking availability, dress code, etcetera. However, for client interaction, unless you know what you say has created nothing but success for you in the past, I encourage you to move away from the notion of pre-scripted dialogue and into understanding the competencies involved in having a great conversation, dancing in open dialogue that is more inquiry-based. Like taking off a heavy pack after hiking uphill for hours, it can be very freeing. Those who use scripts will suggest taking a script and making it your own, which makes sense. However, for some of us that idea of then using the refined script as a means to commencing dialogue seems a bit short on spontaneous authenticity, doesn't it?

My invitation to you is to be open to embracing how you can perform equally well in spontaneous, fearless, genuine conversation without an over-burdening attachment to specific outcome. Open, free-flowing dialogue versus a presentation monologue.

Scripts are a tool. Learn the essence of the messaging contained in them and use your own words in conversation.

Show up authentically and be present in the moment with openness and curiosity.

In the world of acting, script writers are of fundamental importance. Along with other elements, they skillfully craft dialogue. Actors are expected to learn these words and deliver them flawlessly, while exhibiting certain visual behaviours and actions. Actors are typically portraying another person rather than themselves. As agents, are we trying to be someone else? I hope not; we are who we are. Instead of worrying about who we should be or trying to be a person we are not, are we not best served by embracing who we are and working from an inner drive using our own voice?

Take heart from the thousands of professional coaches around the world who dance in free-spirited and instinctive conversation with their clients and are able to seamlessly draw out client-elicited solutions. It can absolutely be done!

They say buyers are liars?

Really? This aged industry expression can occasionally be heard from an agent to describe buyers who keep changing their minds, and it is very interesting to me. "First they told me they wanted X and now they want Y. Last week it was W. They keep moving the goalposts on me!"

It is an unfortunate expression. Are they liars, seriously, because they are taking you all over the place in their search for a home? Or has the agent failed to build and sustain a powerful working partnership, where dialogues are open, and the agent works together with the buyers as a team toward refining their search area? I suspect this is an easy one for you to answer. As consumers, we have every right to take our time and adjust our search parameters. It is the agent's job to partner, collaborate, and guide. No, it is not always easy, but that is why the industry offers healthy compensation in return for our expertise.

It is similar in a way to the common situation where a couple set out in their search for a home with an agent with a shared belief that they are clear on what they want. The agent then proceeds to find a home that meets all the criteria originally set out, yet the couple cannot come to a decision because it no longer meets their changing expectations. For a less experienced agent, this can be difficult to deal with. They cannot understand how the "perfect home" is not eliciting an offer from their buyers. "I just don't get it. That home was exactly what they told me they wanted!"

This is where the sharing of observation can be very helpful. Good examples of this are:

- "Would you mind if I provide a perspective on what I see happening here?"

- "Can I have your permission to share what I am noticing here?"

When we search for a new car, we might visit an auto mall and browse a number of makes and models. Perhaps we want a hatchback and don't even think about whether it has front, rear, or all-wheel drive. We want something that fits our incomplete vision. A door opens and there it is, perfect, right in the colour you wanted. But is it actually the vehicle that fits your intended lifestyle, or does it just look good? You're a skier and visiting local mountains is what you hope to do in the winter months, yet on this vehicle four-wheel drive is only available on a higher model that is more expensive and has features you don't really want. It doesn't make sense, so you decide against that one and leave the dealership unaware at that point as to who has the vehicle that closest meets your needs.

Same with how the home-buying process can begin—a rough idea of requirements but a lack of geographic awareness can take a buyer all the way out of town and out into the valley or up to the mountains.

How can we help these buyers in terms of building awareness? Is it a case of us giving our opinions and telling them what we think could work best for them, or would a deep and probing conversation about lifestyle, future family plans, distance to work, and so on add more value? A good objective is to be able to differentiate yourself from the long list of your competitors who are just happy to take buyers at their word based on solution-based questioning and start immediately looking for what they have been told.

Of course, we can share our opinions and advice—that is part of what we do—but a journey to the source of the objective first and the solutions second may well be more effective, now and in the long run.

So, when *is* it a presentation?

There are many occasions when a traditional presentation makes complete sense. Imagine a convention with three hundred people, and the speaker is trying to have a conversation involving all participants one by one—it makes no sense whatsoever. Materials that corroborate the specific topic that the speaker is talking about, such as a PowerPoint presentation or perhaps a video, are great ways to present a topic and both demonstrate and share expertise.

A situation where some key facts must be conveyed to a group or individuals in a certain timeframe is also perfect for one-way presentation. "Here's what you need to know about this case," or "What we know about this topic so far is ..."

Looking at this from the standpoint of an agent meeting a potential client or perhaps a couple in a living room, why again would we assume that these clients want us to *present*? Once again there's that traditional training methodology and continued attachment to those two rather aged real estate industry expressions—yes, we know: listing presentation and buyer presentation.

It is important to hammer this message home. We are in an industry that constantly *presents*. It seems we love to promote our achievements and celebrate them more than in most other professional fields. Some amongst us who have achieved recognition for sales performance wear that badge as though that is a critical factor. In most cases, it is likely not. It is about who we are and how we show up, and, critically, staying in tune with societal adjustments to communication. Take all of the great reasons behind why consumers choose to work with you, the ones you already understand, and keep up that great work. I would also like to encourage you to add a new element, an invisible file that you carry around with you that you take out anytime you are with your clients, friends, or prospects, a file called *curiosity*.

If you accidentally leave that curiosity file at home, guess what? You'll show up differently and revert back to *present* and *tell* mode. More about that later.

Communication options

In an earlier section I touched on the options available to us now as real estate professionals. Who would have thought thirty years ago that we'd be signing contracts digitally? Everything today is so fast, so immediate, so available. We are challenged by expectation from consumers to answer our phones at all hours (by managing expectations you can go a long way to finding balance with that one).

We have been through times when multitasking was hailed as a great way to go, whereby we can focus on lots of different things at any given time. Is it really? I have spoken with many people who have decried this belief that you can accomplish many things in unison. It makes it difficult to concentrate on anything, so you can end up flitting between working on a document, checking your phone, looking at texts or emails, checking out the weather, sports and social media updates ... and on goes the list of endless multitasking possibilities. What happens when we actually devote our time to focus in on one specific thing?

Focus. Our time. On one. Specific thing. Out of the window flies distraction and in through the front door comes real presence, active listening, and a high level of curious awareness. Is this how we can best serve our clients? Ourselves? Our businesses?

For the sake of awareness and some humour for our Millennials—and to provide some fun reminiscence for others—I think back to my travelling days and how limited our options for communication were, pre-Internet and mobile phone. In 1989, my brother Tim was visiting Canada from England, and his timing was such that we hoped to meet up in Toronto around a certain date that he would be arriving by air from London. I was travelling east, coast to coast, from Vancouver to Halifax by car, and our arrangement was that whoever arrived first would leave a message for the other at the *poste restante*—the general delivery—in the central post office there in Toronto. If you haven't driven coast to coast, let me share with you: it is quite a drive. By the time I arrived in Toronto and picked up his message at the poste restante desk, he was already on his way out. His message said he'd likely be heading west and seeing me in Vancouver in a few weeks. Other than letters, with no fixed addresses due to the travel we didn't really have other options to communicate. Imagine that. Sounds unbelievable today!

These days, we are awash with communication options and, because they are so incredibly efficient and easy to use, they also create another challenge for us. Think about it—is there a price we pay for efficiency?

Back in the day, communication with our real estate clientele was handled in person or by phone, fax, or mail. Add in Internet, email, social media, and the other options of today, is it any wonder that sometimes we get confused as to which medium is best to use? Seasoned professionals consistently share with me that they use many forms of communication with the clients in their databases, which almost always lead toward some quality face-to-face time at a future point.

I have also asked different experienced agents how they would use an extra work hour each day if they were able to have one. Interestingly, the most common response is that they would use that hour to be present with someone in their database. There's that human-connection piece again. Technology comes at us from all angles and demands our attention constantly. However, the one traditional form of communication that remains vitally important is time spent person to person.

Take a step back and think about how you are communicating. Are you generating enough one-on-one time? When you are with these important people in your life, are you really going to do most of the talking? Is your aim really to *present* (as the industry teaches?), or are you curious in the most genuine way?

In terms of face-to-face, there was a great ending to that travel story. A week later, I was sitting in a window nook in a wonderful international beer bar around 7:30 p.m. on a Sunday evening in beautiful Old Quebec. As I raised my glass of beer, I said to myself, "I wonder where Tim is now?" I had a sip, looked across the road, and there he was, looking in a shop window! In a country the size of Canada! You could not script a better look of utter shock and surprise on his face as he turned around. It was brilliant. It was spontaneous. It was a reminder that, even with limited communication options, face-to-face is the absolute best.

Today in your real estate business you likely employ a number of promotional strategies that aim to get you face to face with potential new clients. When that happens, our earlier topic of focusing in to enable active listening through a fundamentally unencumbered presence and an open curiosity clicks in. How does that show up as an example in a dialogue? Here we have an example of "tell versus ask," and in the simplest of terms:

"So, here's what I'd like to do: if you can show me around the home, I'd then like to tell you what I believe it is worth and how I will market it."

Versus...

"What would you like to get out of our conversation today?"

Which one builds trust and authenticity and appeals on an emotional level? Which one builds a valuable collaboration?

Take a step forward—if we are able to refine *presentation* into *conversation*, we then extend an invitation to *partner*. As we identified earlier in the framework, partnering with your clients is a tremendous foundation upon which to build a successful working relationship.

So, the next time you're preparing to meet a potential client, ask yourself, "Am I going to enjoy engaging in a meaningful conversation, or just *present* what I want?" And make sure you have a conversation about what great and efficient communication looks like from their perspective, and share your own perspective, too. It's not going to be a good communication option to send automatic emails of potentially suitable listings to a buyer if they don't prefer to use email. On the other hand, they might prefer a quick text or a call.

Bring perspective into the forefront of your thinking. Ask yourself how you believe you can most effectively communicate with your specific client and then check in with them by asking what works best from their perspective. "Am I sensing that you'd prefer me to pick up the phone and call you if an ideal listing comes onto the market?"

Summary of core principles and self-reflection

Our Learning objectives were to understand:
- **The power of *collaborating* versus *telling***
- **The essence of coaching as a process**
- **How to reframe our thinking on presentations**
- **The difference between using predetermined scripts and spontaneous conversation**
- **How to simply define what the conversation is about**

Bearing in mind all these conversation and presentation perspectives, think about how you can apply some of these principles in the work you do. What opportunities are there if you reframe and refine your interactions with clients?

As usual, some good questions to ask yourself as good reference points:

Operational mode:
What are your actual values?

How spontaneously do you present material?

Can you articulate your value in a non-presentation way that differentiates you from others?

Do you *present to* or *engage with*?

Conversational mode:
Do you typically handle objections in order to win, or actively and authentically engage clients as partners with their concerns?

Do you tend to focus on solution-based closing questions, or do you aim for client-generated solutions?

Do you adequately address communication options with your clients?

Do you use scripts?

What's behind the scenes for you?
Do you really believe that the benefits of multi-tasking outweigh the downside?

What action steps within your control are required to stimulate powerful conversations and help enact meaningful change and better empowered client decisions?

Section 5

Mastering the Conversational Contract

What does it mean to actually *engage*? What effect can it have when we are able to work as a team in the journey from initial conversation of discovery all the way through to possession of a new home?

Learning objectives are to understand:
- **The vitality of the "conversational contract"**
- **How to open up and explore the most relevant topics**
- **How to establish a meeting agenda that brings you together with the client**
- **Building value with the "conversational check-in"**
- **The power and value of paraphrasing**
- **How important the words and vernacular we use in communication are**

A conversational contract—what is *that*?

In the midlands area of England, there is a place fondly called "Spaghetti Junction." Well, perhaps not so fondly. It is basically a challenging jungle of major and minor roads that intersect and require some careful navigation. There are many different directions you can choose to go, and it is probably important not to lose focus or you're heading the wrong way and will need to come back. Having both the driver and perhaps one of the passengers on the same page before you enter will bring the required clarity about how to navigate this to best effect.

Mastering the conversational contract is actually a huge piece of the effective coaching conversation. This means determining what the focus of the conversation will be and can only happen if some great questions are asked and the client is gently challenged.

Here's an illustration of what we're talking about. In one of my group coaching sessions, the conversation started out something like this:

"So, what's on your mind?"

"I need to build my business and I am thinking I need to invest about $3,000 in a new computer and get a better website. That's what I'd like to talk about."

"Okay, so why is it important to you to make that investment?"

"I want to generate more business from online sources."

"How much of your past business has come from online?"

"Very little, actually. Now I think about it, nearly all my business comes from my sphere of influence and referrals."

"Thanks for sharing that. I am curious: on a scale of one to ten, how do you rate the job you are doing in terms of business development with your sphere of influence to date?"

"Hmm ... good question. I would give myself about a five out of ten."

"Looking ahead, what would you like that figure to be?"

"At least an eight or a nine."

"Thinking this through, is it fair to say that there is lots of potential for improvement within an area that is already generating most of your business?"

"Absolutely."

"So, as you reflect on building your business, is it about investing $3,000 in a new computer and going after online business, or are you more interested in mastering an area that is already producing positive results?"

"Wow, I never really thought of that. Yes, it is not about what I first said; I am more interested in finding out how I can communicate better and develop more business from my sphere of influence. That is what I'd like to talk about!"

"Okay. So, what specifically would you like to walk away with from this conversation?"

"Great question! I would like to have three new ideas for how I can improve from a five to an eight or nine."

"So three new ideas ... anything else?"

"No, that would be great. Where do we start?"

If the coach had taken the topic as stated to be about the new computer purchase and the building of online expertise, then the conversation would have moved quickly into possible solutions to fit. Yet, having asked several thought-provoking questions that challenged the agent to think it through, less than two minutes later we are contracting a completely different focus for the conversation, and we know exactly what the coach needs to deliver to generate value.

You might be wondering, "When does the coach give the agent the three ideas?" Ideally, he or she does not. Depending on the skills of the coach, the goal should be to inspire client-generated solutions by coaching the client through the topic. Here's some examples of questions to ask that will help the agent along that path, in no particular order:

"So, can you describe your present communication plan?"

"What can you identify as missing pieces of the puzzle?"

"What impact will it have on your overall business if you really master this communication plan?"

"If there is one thing you would do differently, what might that be?"

It is important to understand that a great coaching conversation is not a linear path. It is a dance that involves many different twists and turns yet hits upon certain core competencies that together ensure a valuable experience and an outcome involving action steps and accountability to match.

When we adopt a solution-based approach, it seems easier. There we are, answering exactly what the client has asked for—how ideal is that? However, the challenge is that we are not helping our client identify something else that may be more important to focus in on. Maybe there isn't anything else; if that is the case, it will become apparent pretty quickly and you can then proceed as requested, because that is clearly the best way forward at that point for you and the client.

Here's another perspective: have you ever been looking at a product, a new car or a new computer, or contracting for some financial advice, and been stumped by questions to ask the salesperson? With the car, we look inside, we sit inside, we look at the curves and lines. We might cast an eye over the specifications and fuel-economy details, but we're still not really sure what we should be asking. So a question might just pop into mind, such as: "What can you tell me about the engine?" when in fact you are not actually that interested in the engine. The salesperson takes the question and likely gives us a full rundown on the aspects of the power plant they know about and things that they might have opinions about. So, what could the salesperson do to help the buyer? Perhaps ask some questions such as: "What kind of lifestyle will your car be serving?" or "What kind of things do you use a car for, typically?" In essence, he could employ a coaching approach to find out what's really important to the car buyer.

Opening up the options for conversation is an art developed over time. When you are able to refine the conversational contract, it can be very powerful for the recipient and focus the dialogue in a meaningful way.

Uncovering the real topic for you and your client to focus on

In my sales career, I had a client I worked with for probably two to three years. The net result was that they ended up renovating the same house they had lived in for years. I failed to see what later became obvious—that there was not really a clear decision-maker. Not only that, the husband was not invested in actually moving; he was happy staying where they were. It was usually the same pattern: as the wife worked and he was the house dad, he would be the one to preview homes with me. Every so often we'd be out looking at a property or two as they came onto the market, followed sometimes by a coffee or a lunch. He was an awesome guy and I always enjoyed the time and conversation. A number of times we viewed a home for the second time with his wife and kids in tow. "We'll get back to you" was often the response to the interest they had shown, and we saw a number of homes that actually matched what they wanted on paper.

The real topic was essentially that it was the wife who was really the one who liked these better homes, and, over time, it became clearer that he was the one influencing decisions or dissuading a purchase. In addition, he really found it next to impossible to move on from where they lived, hence the renovation that followed some time later.

Looking back, I could easily have uncovered these factors and challenged them for mutual benefit, had I understood the importance of authentically partnering with them through the challenge of making a decision to move or stay and taken the time to guide them. I was blinded by the pleasure I took in spending time with this great guy and also the size of potential commissions when a decision was made. They were a pleasure to be with, lovely people, and in the end, their best decision was to stay where they were. In the sense of helping them refine that thinking, I am glad to have played that part.

Let's get into how we can help ourselves and our clients determine what the focus of the conversation should be. Here it is important to take some time to look at five absolute keys behind the ability to focus your client in on a specific conversational topic. Here goes …

Guide your client to open up and explore the conversation by getting some balls up in the air!

When we go shopping, we tend to like having a selection of products to choose from. Let's say you're searching for a new pair of shoes. Do you buy the first pair you look at? Not typically. We tend to appreciate a range to choose from, as that adds value to the process and cements our commitment to buying one particular pair by refining the choices.

How a conversation unfolds has so many possibilities. It can be ineffective and out of focus, or it can be highly effective and laser-focused.

As a conversational partner, is your role to lead such a conversation? Maybe. What happens if we reframe *lead* to *guide*?

As a conversational guide, we can walk alongside our client without the need to lead. In fact, the only real leading that needs to take place is procedural—making sure that we partner with our client to achieve what is needed from that conversation, and any potential contractual paperwork that might follow.

Think about how you can guide the conversation, and how you can be of best service and add the most value for your client. What if you are able to shine a light on what they actually want and need to get out of the conversation?

Let that sit for a moment—we can't help but make assumptions, which are perhaps based on a preceding conversation that you had with the client when you set up the appointment. In presentation mode, our own assumptions or directives can actually do a disservice to whomever is sitting there across from us. Here's an example of the former versus the latter:

"So, Terry, you said on the phone that you would like to know what your home is worth as you might be interested in selling it—so why don't you show me around?"

"Okay."

Versus:

"So, Terry, you shared with me on the phone that you would like to know what your home is worth as you might be interested in selling it. I am curious—what's driving those thoughts?"

"To be honest, it looks like I am being laid off at work so we're looking at options."

"I am very sorry to hear that. Would it be helpful if we explored what options there might be?"

"Actually, that would be helpful. We are feeling very stressed right now."

The agent now engages the client in a deeper discussion that is centred upon *his* needs instead of the agent's needs of seeing the property—that comes later.

Both approaches can work; however, ask yourself which one will do a better job of building partnership with the clients. By engaging with how someone is feeling instead of what they are thinking, an agent will likely increase her chances of being the one selected to work with. The beginning of the interaction offers the added benefit of making a resounding first impression.

In this example, the other person feels heard and understood and this style communicates empathy and active listening.

When I am listening in to a group-coaching conversation, where a number of people are coaching one person, I listen for these balls being thrown into the air. Or the imagery of releasing balloons into the air helps me think about the options for conversation that are being generated.

Refining focal points for the conversation

Knowing that we normally tend to take what people say at face value—they ask specifically for one thing and so we deliver on that one thing—how can we not jump to the conclusion that what someone says he is interested in talking about actually is what he wants to focus the conversation on? From a professional coaching perspective, it is essential to refine the options and determine a clarity of focus.

The earlier examples I have provided show that within three to five quality questions you can drill down into what is important for the client, and then help them refine what needs to float up to the surface as a main topic. It doesn't mean it is the only topic, but it is the one that receives full attention as a priority.

So, going back to our magical piece here, as options are coaxed out in conversation and a number of balls are thrown up in the air (they are *not* for the coach to catch), the magic is to have the client select one and then catch it. This then becomes the main topic to move forward with.

"We're thinking of selling our house and want to know what it is worth in your opinion, as well as whether or not now is the right time to sell it."

"Okay, great. Would you like to show me around? Then we can talk about the value."

Versus:

"We're thinking of selling our house and want to know what it is worth in your opinion, as well as whether or not now is the right time to sell it."

"Great, I'm hearing that you are curious about your home's value and also market conditions. What else is there?"

"Hmm. I guess we're thinking about moving to the Island, but we're not quite sure yet."

"Okay, so maybe a conversation around lifestyle goals—would that be helpful?"

"Yes, absolutely. We want to move, but we're not sure quite where ... we just feel we've been here long enough. Oh, also the upstairs carpets are in rough shape; should we be changing them?"

"Okay, so we can have a conversation that includes the current market conditions, what's driving your thoughts of moving, your lifestyle, your carpets, and then the current value. Which one of those would you like to start with?"

This effectively puts five balls up in the air, followed by an invitation to your client to catch one of them. That is guidance in motion, isn't it?

The agenda—whose is it?

This really is where even more magic can—and hopefully will—happen!

Our objective above is to skillfully guide the conversation so that a topic can be discovered, refined, and focused upon, based on what the client is spontaneously bringing to the conversation. This process of opening up and exploring applies equally when we think about setting meeting agendas.

In traditional engagements, our eagerness to turn up to the meeting organized and in control sometimes means we set an agenda in advance of the meeting, putting forward what we believe needs to be discussed, sometimes without reference or invitation to what the client might want from the interaction.

I recall a conversation with an agent during one of my courses—I asked if anyone likes to set an agenda prior to meeting a potential buyer or seller. His hand shot up.

I asked how that process works and he described how he sits down and produces a pre-written agenda that outlines what they will talk about in the meeting. This helped him feel organized and business-like. I then asked the group whether they felt the client or themselves should set the agenda. With hands going up on both sides, I encouraged thoughts of a third option: a *shared* agenda. What if you were to co-create an agenda right there in the meeting by collaborating with the client? This was met with positive nods, as the partnership penny slotted gently into place.

"So, you mean we don't go in with a pre-determined structure; we co-develop it with the client?"

"Yes!"

As this agent considered this, he enthusiastically shared how much he liked that idea, how it would release him of the burden of having to develop an agenda on his own, and how it could help him be more present and provide even more value. That sounded like a win to me. In subsequent groups, it has been met with almost unanimous support.

Four brilliant partnering questions to establish a high-value agenda

You are in the living room, engaged in relaxed get-to-know-you type of dialogue with the homeowner, what our industry terms "building rapport." All good. Then you begin the invitation to a shared agenda. This might go something like this (note the questions in bold):

"So now we have gotten to know each other a bit more, **what would you like to get out of our conversation** this morning, John?"

"Hmm. I'd like to know what you think my place is worth, how the market is, how long you think it will take to sell."

"Great, thanks for sharing that. **Is there anything else?**"

"Yeah, I am also wondering what you think about changing the upstairs carpets, they are really old."

"Okay, so four things from your perspective there. Value of your home, the market, how much time it will take to sell, and the upstairs carpets."

"Yes, bang on."

"**Can I share what I would like to get out of the conversation?** I would like to find out what attracted you most to buying this home and also have a discussion about your next goal of buying in the Okanagan."

"Okay, sounds good."

"Excellent. **Which one would you like to start with**?"

As the agent, you have guided the conversation and identified six topics. By inviting your homeowner to select the one they want to start with, you are really engaging them. I would also recommend you write down each topic as they first arise, so that you can both see the agenda as it unfolds.

If you believe in the essence of partnership and are committed to playing that guiding role as well as possible, how can you refine your current process of establishing an agenda?

During one of my classes, I received some amazing feedback from an Agent who came from an extensive and successful corporate training background. Hearing me deliver the question "what would you like to get out of the conversation today?" his response was "that's the most significant, impactful question I have heard in the last five years." Sometimes what sounds and seems so easy can serve to instantly drive the partnership process and drill into the core of what's important to the client.

The check-in during a long conversation

Being in an industry that has traditionally involved a *present* and *tell* type of dialogue, one of the components of exploring the real topic is to check in periodically. This is important for several reasons, that include:

- Is the client getting what they need from the conversation?

- Is there something more pressing that the client needs to unpack?

So, the phraseology that can go along with this might be:

"Can we have a quick check-in? How is our conversation landing so far with you?"

Or:

"Can we pause for a moment? Is there anything more pressing that you need us to focus in on right now?"

We're all human and we all experience a wandering mind on occasion. It is quite possible that we lose the plot and can't even remember where we are in a conversation. Oops! That's okay, the beauty of coaching includes an ability to get back on track without necessarily exposing your wandering thoughts. This might sound like:

"Just a quick check-in—where do you feel we are in the conversation right now?"

Here are what I believe to be six values for checking in during conversation:

- It ensures relevancy
- It invites acknowledgement of value being received by the client, or otherwise
- It speaks to engaging in partnership
- It makes sure you are mutually accountable to keeping the conversation moving forward and on track
- It helps identify if there is something else that is coming up in your client's mind
- It provides an opportunity to share something else that you want to bring attention to

Check-ins versus pronouncement

Thinking back, can you remember being in class with a teacher or professor who just completely resonated with you? For me, such a man is Norm Amundsen, author of many great works, including *The Physics of Living* and *Active Engagement: The Being and Doing of Career Counselling*. One extremely valuable tip that I learned from this is the notion of establishing a clear theme at the beginning of a conversation and then revisiting it throughout the dialogue. This is what we call the "check-in" to the "conversational contract" that we have established together.

Sometimes we think we're doing fine and a conversation is humming along beautifully. At least, that is how it seems from our perspective. After all, we have been asking brilliant questions, listening intently, paraphrasing in nuggety fashion, and having a warm and engaging presence. Our mind seems to be on coaching autopilot—even though we are being completely spontaneous and authentic—and we are flicking through the gears and moving along in partnership with our client. Is it true? Or might we be making a (*gasp*) assumption?

Check in periodically to find out. *Pronounce* at your peril! So, here are a couple of illustrations for how these conversations might transpire. First, a listing conversation:

"Jane, I am really enjoying this conversation. We're making real progress."

"Well, I am glad you feel that way, because I don't."

"Oh, really? I thought we were moving things along really well, no?"

"We've been talking all about your marketing plan, but I am not even totally sure if now is the right time to sell my home."

Versus:

"Jane, can we pause for a few moments? I'd like to hear where you feel we are in our conversation so far."

"Well, thanks for asking. Would it be okay if we held off on talking about marketing details and such? I am not even totally sure if now is the right time to sell my home."

"Thank you for sharing that. Absolutely, would it be helpful to address the timing aspects of selling, or is there something else that is more pressing for you?"

"Yes, let me think … well, I guess I am wondering if we should hold off until the new year, to see how the market is then?"

"Okay, so let's address timing and market conditions. To be crystal clear, what would you hope to walk away with from that specific conversation?"

"It would be great to actually *make* a decision—list today, or wait."

As you can see, it is vital to open up and explore conversation and then focus it in on specifics and identify what would constitute a clear takeaway. In this example: simply a decision, one that might have been missed completely had the agent kept presenting their marketing plan and so forth. Think about building partnership, one block at a time. Here's another example with a buyer conversation, after a showing:

"Wow, does *that* home ever tick all the boxes, eh?"

"I'm not sure why you're so excited. It just doesn't feel right to me."

"But it's got the view you want, in the price range you want, in a building you want …"

"Yes, but the floorplan doesn't work. Let's keep looking."

"Okay ... [Thinking, *I don't believe it! That home is perfect!*] Let's keep looking, then."

Versus:

"So, what do you think about that home?"

"It certainly had a lot of the things I am looking for, but the floorplan just doesn't feel right to me."

"Okay, to help me better understand that, which part of that floorplan challenges you?"

"It's the way the living room is open to the kitchen like that—I somehow imagined a bit more privacy between the two."

"Apart from that, does the rest of the suite tick all your boxes?"

"Erm ... yes, I guess it does. That's the only question mark I really have."

"I am curious ... what real benefit does having a wall between the rooms provide for you?"

"Privacy, I guess?"

"I remember that this is your number-one building that you'd like to be in, and you mentioned you love the kitchens. They actually get their natural light through the living room windows."

"So that's why they are so open. That makes sense then ..."

They say patience is a virtue. It is a skill and one which is essential in partnership. When we show up without judgement and with a genuine quest to understand, we increase the likelihood of mutual success. But please resist the urge to pronounce your opinions. Another example of that is when someone says, "Oh, I know just how you feel." Really? How can you? We are all different. When you pronounce an opinion, you are imposing your own thoughts into the conversation which might serve to create distance between you and your client. If we are committed to the idea of client-generated solutions, then pronouncing our opinions does not really fit, does it?

Identification of what the client hopes to walk away with from the conversation

If "what would you like to get out of our conversation today" is a great way to start the process of mastering the conversational contract, perhaps equally important is the other bookend that enables you to really deliver value for your client.

"At the end of our conversation, what would you like to walk away with?" This simple and clear question allows your client to describe exactly what they would like you to help them cover. They are giving you a roadmap and description of how you can really help them. How cool is that?

As an example: a client has agreed that the conversational contract is "how to get their home ready to go on the market." There is a ton of work to do and they don't know where to start.

Think about how we can approach this topic. It could be a traditional way:

"Well, shall we list out everything that needs doing?"

Or, it could be through the simple refinement of asking:

"So, how to get your home ready for the market ... what exactly would you like to walk away with from this conversation?"

"A plan for tackling all the deficiencies, the painting and carpeting work. Maybe a list I can follow and check off as things get done."

"Okay, that's clear. So, what's the first thing on the list?"

"How about garbage removal and clear-up?"

As the conversation gains momentum, the agent has a choice to make:

- Choose to *lead* the conversation, making suggestions and giving ideas along the way (the risk being that the non-client generated solutions receive less buy-in)

- Choose to *guide* the conversation by drawing out from the client each step required and their action plan (client-generated, so more chance they will follow through)

What an opportunity! By engaging, asking, and collaborating, our approach aligns you with your client and is in harmony with the partnership framework. Your patience is rewarded through a list of action steps and timelines, and accountability is achieved by asking the client to identify who is responsible for each piece, by when, and any impact of not achieving them.

When it is clear what your client needs from you, it builds your circumstantial confidence and sets up a high-quality professional interaction—one that has a higher likelihood of building trust and confidence for your client in you and how you work.

Paraphrasing

This is a highly valuable tool to help reflect back to someone the basic gist of what they have been saying, all the way through to identifying the golden nuggets. Paraphrasing uses key words that are heard by the recipient in a reflective way and it provides for succinct summarization of what a client is telling you. It also enables you to memorize what you are hearing by playing it back to your client in slightly different words, and it empowers the spirit of partnership.

By its very essence, it is engaging because it demands active listening to everything that is being said (and a sense of what might not be said). It also provides a perfect entry point for a deeper P1 or P2 type of question.

"I'm hearing that you've had the home listed before with two different agents and it has not resulted in a sale— what's behind that, from your perspective?"

"Well, they just didn't get buyers to come and see it."

"That could be a reason. What else could result in potential buyers choosing not to view the home?"

"It can't be the price!"

"I'm sensing you believe your asking price is attractive enough to entice buyers. What if you challenge that thinking?"

"How?"

"Well, I've heard that neither of two agents over a ten-month period could attract many potential buyers, and certainly no offers. You believe your price is attractive and we know that homes are selling in this balanced market. What if we re-examine our asking price from the viewpoint of a buyer actively looking to buy, and see what we can see?"

Paraphrasing is so important that, in its absence, we tend to just dive straight into a topic and ask lots of questions without necessarily having a clear picture of everything we need to surface. Back to the iceberg analogy—paraphrasing is an important element in helping us get into what's below the waterline, together.

Paraphrasing provides an opportunity to:

- Ensure that you are not missing anything
- Provide validation for your client through your acute listening
- Build your partnership
- Ask and land a powerful, thought-provoking question

Used in combination with active listening and powerful questions, paraphrasing has the power and potential to move the conversation forward as partners, especially when some silence provides thinking space for your client.

Reflect back to your childhood!

We touched on this earlier. Children are amazingly inquisitive by nature. As any parent will attest to, they are constantly asking questions. Their curiosity abounds. As Norm Amundsen sets out in *The Physics of Living*, a year to a child of two represents 50 percent of their life. To a fifty-year old, that year represents only 2 percent. It seems apparent that adults tend to be less curious and more opinionated, based on all this life experience and the vast knowledge that grows between our ears. So, we actually have to work hard in order to bring back that deep and genuine curiosity that we had as children!

A good place to start is by making a renewed commitment to what we all did from a young age at school—the three L's of learning, listening, and language. What happens as we revitalize our use of these?

As you ponder the foundational elements involved in adjusting how you converse with clients, does it feel exciting to focus in on *learning* these meaningful new competencies? I have seen that many agents adopt a real openness to the learning process of mastering new skills. Every conversational interaction then adds a piece to this valuable and meaningful learning experience. To become familiar with and then more comfortable with the frameworks and lenses to look through is itself a comprehensive and dynamic learning process.

In our day-to-day lives, it is easy to become a victim of distraction. Several thousand marketing messages are aimed at us daily, whether we welcome them or not, and to a large extent we become accustomed to tuning them out. In coaching interactions, the act of actually *listening* is so very powerful and critical to the flow of conversation and the overall coaching experience. Within this coaching context, it feels as though there is a magnifying glass and a spotlight attached to the *listening* aspect of the interaction. It is not possible to tune out for a moment. Fully engaged listening is as important as water to a plant.

And then we have that linguistic term "language" ...

Think about possibilities and the importance of the language we choose to use

In 1967, Albert Mehrabian set out a belief that only 7 percent of communication happens through the words we use, when attitudes and feelings are involved. The rest comprises body language (55 percent) and our tone, cadence, volume, and the way we speak (38 percent). When I first heard this, my initial thought was, *Hmm, I guess what we say is not that important then*, quickly followed by *Actually, the opposite is true—if we only have 7 percent, it is crucial to make sure we use language that lands!*

I absolutely love language and the freedom we enjoy in putting our sentences together as we like. In particular, I enjoy the process of refining powerful questions and choosing language that has the most impact on a conversation. Think about words that deeply resonate for you when you hear or use them. The careful and considered selection of the right words. The very *language* we use determines the response and the ability to bring out someone's values, thoughts, challenges, and goals. It is largely in verbal form; yet, let us not forget the body-language aspect as well and the relevance of posture and mirroring.

So, try to always be mindful of your choice of words; ensure that they are valuable within your coaching style and then just work your linguistic magic. No matter what languages we speak, it is the words and expressions within the language we choose that are crucial. Your vernacular is everything and how you choose to use it can be thought-provoking, creative, inspiring, and fun!

Core coaching concepts—three words I have chosen to help you reflect

Core. Coaching. Concepts. As simple as that! *Core* refers to what is central and essential as a requirement, the fundamentals that form the heart of the matter and which feed the whole system of communication.

Coaching in this realm refers to the basic ability to draw out client-generated solutions by embracing the key operating principles of ask, engage, and collaborate.

Concepts to me refers to the underlying material foundations—in this case the ICF framework and those five enormously important terms that I have drawn out of their definition: partnering, thought-provoking, creative, inspiring, and potential.

Summary of core principles and self-reflection

Our learning objectives were to understand:

- **The vitality of the "conversational contract"**
- **How to open up and explore the most relevant topics**
- **How to establish a meeting agenda that brings you together with the client**
- **Building value with the "conversational check-in"**
- **The power and value of paraphrasing**

- **How important the words and the vernacular we use in communication are**

As you come to terms with the idea of mastering a conversational contract, how you can apply some of these principles in the work you do? Can you identify opportunities to better engage clients?

Here are some good questions to ask yourself as good reference points:

Operational mode:
Do you typically set the agenda for a client meeting? How can that process be improved?

How powerful is the language that you currently use with clients, and how do you know it is resonating?

Conversational mode:
Are you doing the best job possible in helping clients discover their true drivers and needs?

How clear are you on discovering what your client actually wants and needs to get out of a conversation with you?

How do you currently check in to find out if you are truly helping them and not just making an assumption?

What's behind the scenes for you?
Are you the kind of person who cannot resist inserting their own opinions into a conversation?

What, if anything, stands in the way of you making adjustments to how you engage with clients?

What impact could it have on your role if you are able to help your clients refine what is most important for them?

How can you increase your client's perception of your value by mastering a conversational contract?

What action steps within your control are required to stimulate more powerful conversations and help enact meaningful change and better empowered client decisions?

Are you on the way to building deeper, more effective working relationships with your clients?

Section 6

Understanding some of the Structural Elements and your own norms

How do we show up? How can we best equip ourselves and establish a more effective start with clients? What defines our success?

Learning objectives are to understand:
- **The elements of our own professional presence**
- **How to lay a foundation of working harmoniously and effectively together**
- **How we can look at the interview process in a different way**
- **Our skills and what we have in our own tool chests**
- **The power of tapping into feelings**
- **The importance of parking thoughts of entitlement to business**

What does professional presence mean?

In person-based coaching, change occurs once clients start feeling understood, accepted, and comfortable expressing themselves. Those who feel comfortable expressing their true feelings and thoughts are way more likely to change in a positive way. Professional presence can play a vital role in this. Indeed, professional presence and active listening are vital components of successful interpersonal engagements.

Let's briefly review some of the words that speak to professional presence:

Personal: Attire and how you look, hygiene, and personal grooming.

Tools: Clean car, computer, tablet, phone (not ringing away)—all in good working order. Preparedness of all relevant knowledge and spontaneous presentation materials required

Affiliation/Branding: Association with your brokerage brand, consideration given to meeting location

Interpersonal qualities:
- Awareness (cultural/religious)
- Greeting/handshake and general manners
- Body language
- Making eye contact with focus
- Being punctual, present, and attentive
- Politeness and graciousness
- Being welcoming, comforting, and collaborating
- Being engaged through active listening and asking powerful questions
- Establishing a shared agenda
- Holding confidences as required
- Being ethical and acting with integrity
- Paraphrasing effectively
- Use of pauses and silence to enrich the provocation of thought
- Positive non-judgemental attitude
- Mindful curiosity

- Empathy
- Intonation and rate of speech
- Biting your tongue if needed
- Having a strategy for interpersonal engagement and avoiding information overload
- Articulate, calm, and open
- Ability to read your audience
- Political correctness
- Patience and understanding needs
- Using your strengths
- Being engaging, approachable, and respectful
- Use of appropriate gestures/posture
- Resourcefulness and responsiveness
- Being flexible by nature

As these words describe, how your cumulative presence shows up can work either for you or against you. A great place to begin working on how you can show up well and embody these qualities is to review each of them and determine what is required for that important upcoming conversation. When did you last check in on your own presence?

Creating working guidelines with your clients

If we agree that partnering with our clients is a solid objective to work toward, how can we best lay a foundation that supports that goal? When I introduce a new group to a course, we always take the time to encourage input from all members of the group toward identifying what our working guidelines will be for the course. In other words, what do we, as a group, strive to adhere to in creating the most effective environment for mutual engagement, learning, and maximizing the impact we can have for each other?

What if we employ a similar idea with our prospective clients and have a discussion around how we each view working together for best results?

As I reviewed the agreements that various groups made, I thought it would be valuable to share some of the key points that surfaced, so that you can see a picture of what kind of qualities they expected from each other. Here they are:

- Be on time/punctual
- Hold confidences
- Be respectful
- Be curious
- Be engaged
- Ask questions
- Dig deeper and embrace vulnerability
- Be organized and prepared
- Maintain an open mind toward different opinions
- Be supportive and encouraging
- Team vs. individual focus
- Provide constructive feedback
- Create a safe zone and comfortable atmosphere
- Agree to disagree and find a solution
- Shift perspectives
- Start the conversation with something positive
- Exercise honesty/integrity
- Be fair
- Be open
- Bring humour
- Wish others well
- Be transparent
- Listen
- Be factual
- Be tolerant

- Trust in each other
- Be patient
- Be mindful
- Be considerate
- Be professional
- Be authentic
- Make it fun!
- Be accountable
- Be engaged
- Be reliable
- Be passionate
- Stay invested
- Stay on topic
- Be non-judgemental
- Work in the best interests of each other
- No interrupting each other
- Learn from each other
- Apply what we learn!
- Be present
- Fully participate
- Be giving
- Adapt

"How are we supposed to have a discussion like this with a client? What if they don't want that?" I can almost hear your questions coming up ... and I ask you to park those fears and doubts, for good. Here are two simple questions that will help you establish a solid working foundation with any client:

"As we move forward together and start the search for your next home, I am curious about how we can work together most effectively—what would a great working relationship look like to you?"

And:

"Great, now we have taken care of the paperwork, there's one last question I have for you. I am curious—how would you like me to communicate with you? What forms of contact do you prefer—a phone call, email, text, face-to-face? What typically is your preference?" Then "Can I share my preference and what I have found to be most effective with clients?"

As these conversations unfold, be creative. Delve into values, stories of clients or other agents calling you at all hours ... be creative! Giving a client a peek behind the curtain and some insight into what your life as a real estate professional is actually like can build your working relationship and even increase their perception of your value. Use your relationship power instead of your positional power. We assume people know what we do—most times, they only have a vague idea. So, take the time ... these are the types of conversations that can really ground a solid working relationship.

And don't forget to smile! Seriously.

Working with congruence and vision

A potential client has thoughts of buying or selling a home. We have already established many times in this book that, instead of going straight into the *solutions* questions, we are better served by spending some quality time together in P1 or P2. A key message to understand is that progress is not linear, it is like rafting down a meandering river: sometimes you're right in the middle and in full flow, other times your trajectory sets you against rocks or high and dry up on the sand of the riverbank. However, your journey continues along and each of the infinite adjustments brings a new and exciting learning discovery.

To keep the focus person-based and to maximize client buy-in, it is important to maintain the forward momentum by asking great questions and avoiding *telling* at all costs. Great language to use around this could be something like:

"How can we approach this situation so that we come up with some solutions together?"

Congruence is the quality of working in harmony. Vision provides a pathway to the future and inspires imagery for you and your client. The sentence above is a great example of partnership language, and, while it invites solution development together, in its most inspired form these solutions are carefully drawn out from the client by you.

The four stages of learning are *unconscious incompetence, conscious incompetence, conscious competence,* and *unconscious competence.* The pendulum of life swings between unconscious incompetence and conscious competence for all of us. Without coaching, many of us perform to a level that falls far short of what we are capable of. In fact, having a passion to coach a client and help develop their capacity to *do* can be incredibly satisfying. And this is a real opportunity to enrich your working relationships with your clients in our industry. What works well for coaches will work well for your clients, too. Seek to work towards a vision, together in harmony.

Reframing how we approach an interview

Here's another perspective on how coaching principles can be adopted to positively change a conversation. This is an example of what happens when we apply for a job and are awarded an interview.

Sometimes life can serve up just what you have been hoping for and everything seems to be aligning—you've just landed that perfect job opportunity and set a time and date: 2:00 p.m. next Wednesday. What typically happens in the days leading up to that?

As the interview approaches, we can become more and more attached to the outcome: being offered and actually landing the job. We start to think about what it will mean, perhaps the change of fortune it promises, and how our life can be positively impacted. We also tend to become a little anxious and fearful of failure, don't we? That "what if I flop and can't answer the questions I am presented with" kind of negative self-talk that can creep its way in. There's the fear of not wanting to let down family members and friends you have told about the pending interview, of not wanting to let yourself down...

I witnessed this first-hand during a class. There were about forty of us, and one of the class leads shared her exciting news of an upcoming interview for a dream job the following week. That next day she expressed to us that by sharing this interview news with the whole class, she had actually ramped up the pressure on herself. She shared that she had felt this self-imposed pressure, as she'd now have to report back in with everyone at a future class about her interview success or lack thereof, and didn't want to disappoint us if she didn't land the job. As she talked her challenge through, she voiced to us that it helped her release some of that pressure, yet I was sensing that she was still burdened by it. So, I picked a quiet moment to approach and ask her one simple question:

"Where are you going on Thursday?"

"The interview."

"Sorry, what are you going to be doing?"

"Having an appointment?" she asked quizzically, and then, with a little moment of self-realization that I was able to coax from her, she said, "Having a conversation!"

Aha! The penny had dropped. She went on to say how much lighter she was feeling and thanked me for that simple mindset adjustment. She shared with me how seeing it that way was relieving for her, without any attachment to expectation. Indeed, the only outcome she committed to was to have a good conversation.

I use the word "incremental" a lot—that slight adjustment in what we say or how we think that can create a large impact compared to the size of the adjustment.

If we can have confidence in the conversation itself and employ that confidence as a means of connecting well, then we are better able to relax, be more focused and present, and really shine. In this case, as we discussed, she didn't at that point have that position and life was still good anyway.

Being apprehensive or concerned pales in value to being free to shine on the day. By making such a mindset adjustment, you can focus on enjoying the challenge and the experience. This then provides a solid foundation to participate as a valued partner in the conversation.

Are you wondering what the outcome of that interview was? Here's some feedback from that interviewee:

"The impact our brief conversation had on the interview was quite large and impactful. You were able to help me reframe so that my focus became the conversation and not the outcome, the family, the class. I was able to get rid a lot of the 'what ifs' getting in the way. I remember making a comment to my husband after our conversation about how helpful that was. I also had a great interview, and I was offered the job the day after. So, great outcome."

Let's look at what can unfold in an interview conversation. It's probably safe to say that all of us, at one time or another, have felt we could have performed better when applying for a job, a university, or a course.

"How was the interview?"

"Um, it could have gone a lot better. I was nervous, and I don't think I answered all the questions well enough."

This type of scenario suggests an imbalance between interviewer and interviewee, the "power over" imbalance we talked about earlier being very apparent throughout— and likely felt on the receiving end by the applicant.

Yet think about a scenario where there are multiple applicants for a position and one really stands out and performs well at interview. Does that same "power over" imbalance still apply? It could, but it is unlikely to be anywhere near as pronounced.

Let's say a second person also performed well at an interview. Maybe their resumé was not quite as polished or their experience not quite as deep as the first candidate, but something about them really stood out and started laying building blocks of a partnership with the interviewer. You might be wondering how that can happen.

If interviewees dedicate themselves to losing attachment to anything other than having a good conversation and asking some questions that land well, they will incrementally increase their chances of performing well and standing out from the crowd.

Having enjoyed the privilege of being in the same room with hundreds of candidates entering the real estate field over the years, I have seen both ends of the spectrum. At one extreme, a candidate says very little and virtually only speaks when presented with a question. At the other end of the spectrum, they show up relaxed and engaged, and provide me with a deep and meaningful conversational experience that has been loaded with their questions and genuine curiosity and expressed in ways that challenge me to answer. As they ask me the great questions, I ask them back. What develops is a high-value conversation that can only come through a shared curiosity—from both sides of the table.

I have heard agents tells others that "a listing or buyer presentation is just like a job interview: you have to make a great impression." If we can reframe that thinking in terms of losing attachment to outcome and focusing instead on the quality and depth of the conversation, then we will show up in a more inspired and differentiating manner.

In the brokerage I have been associated with, we refer to these interviews as "mutual fit assessments." This contrasts with how some brokerages choose to use the traditional "let me tell you all about us" type of approach that is higher on selling and lower on curiosity as to who they are selling to. Is it a recruiting strategy? Or is it an attraction strategy? There is a big difference.

Let's look at two of the major differences between how compensation plans are structured by brokerages—a split of commissions based on sales success and fixed monthly fees that are payable every month. If the plan is based purely on a split structure, where the brokerage's success is entirely dependent upon that of its agents and monthly fees are not charged, then how important is it to attract agents whom the brokerage believes will be successful and whom they can help guide that success for? If the brokerage model has no split and instead charges fixed monthly fees, then the dynamic shifts to reduced dependency on agent success. So is there then the same need to focus on who is sitting across the table? Both models have their merits and brokerages tend to offer structures commensurate with the level and value of support services they offer.

A real estate agent interview to join a brokerage actually shares similarities with an agent meeting with a potential seller or buyer. Which side of the ledger would you rather be on, *selling* and *telling*, or *attracting* and *asking*? You have a choice, absolutely. It is not for me to tell you which is best for you. However, I do extend an invitation to adapt and refine a more modern alternative that might over time send "*present* and *tell*" to the same place as the fax machine and the cassette tape player …

Instead of viewing your next buyer or seller appointment as a presentation and an interview, can I encourage you to reframe it as a natural conversation? Do you find that sounds a bit more appealing?

Redefining our interpretation of hard skills

Part of what comprises "hard skills" are the knowledge of policies, procedures, and factual information. Another part is what you should say to clients and how you should hold a dialogue. That's the part I'd like to address: the words "should" and "how."

For years, trainers have said, "You need a combination of hard skills and soft skills to be successful in sales." I have said the same and shared that belief myself. Today, I am challenging that thinking and I believe it is necessary to redefine hard skills.

Traditional interpretations in the deepest sense might include scripts and closed dialogues. The "this is what you should say in this situation" kind of approach. Do you believe in scripts and dialogues, and handling objections by having a pre-scripted answer? Sure, there are some occasions when they might be helpful, but are they always the most effective option? How do we feel when we are on the receiving end of a canned approach?

My sense is that the line between hard skills and soft skills is blurring. I see *asking* and *engaging* as valid replacements for *telling* and *presenting*, and that these are themselves becoming hard skills.

While I acknowledge that we all have our own definitions of what hard skills are, another interpretation of hard skills are the mentoring aspects of what we do—our expertise with contracts, clauses, marketing, how we hold open houses, how we put together and maintain a database, our system, and so on. Every business has some hard skills to it.

But I do not believe that the hard skills of the future include the traditional scripts and dialogues methodology—the "they say that, so I say this" kind of approach.

When soft skills and hard skills combine to be an ongoing conversational landscape that covers everything from the valley (motivations, desires, drivers) to the mountaintop (best case scenarios, fabulous solutions, results mutually achieved), then we will have performed professionally for our clients and helped them reach their goals without the need for traditional sales techniques and those old hard skills. The "how" is all about the framework of the conversation.

What's in your tool belt and tool chest?

If we think about the construction industry, there are handymen who have skills in a great many areas and choose not to specialize in only one. If a client is building a house, they don't typically seek out a handyman, but a collection of professional tradespeople who each have a distinct skillset that they bring to the overall project.

As real estate professionals, we are that same handyman in many ways—we need to understand bookkeeping, negotiation, marketing, the running of a business ... yet we also need to have distinct skill sets that resonate with our clients.

Coaching is an art and a science. Rule out complacency, it is an art that you can only master over a long period and with great patience. Even the most experienced coaches recognize that they can learn more and build greater skills each day, that there is no ceiling. The art can be in ascertaining and mastering as much as possible certain tools that work really well for you.

So, what do you have in your tool belt?

Tradespeople often carry a tool belt, which contains the tools they need to use the most. Behind the scenes, many have another supply of equipment that they can call into action if needed for a specific task.

As agents, let's just say that our basic tool belt contains:

- A tape measure
- Professional disclosures, documents, and files
- Technology (computer, phone, etc.)
- Market knowledge
- Negotiation skills

What else can you keep in your tool chest?

And what enabling skills and benefits do these extra tools bring to the profession? Here are six suggestions to add to yours:

❑ **That file called *curiosity***

Being genuinely curious, no matter who we are meeting with or why

❑ **Commitment to spontaneous presentation**

Are you willing to adjust the notion of listing or buyer presentation?

❑ **Mindfulness and preparation techniques**

What are you committing to moving forward, in terms of being in the very best mindset you can be in for the most important upcoming business appointments? What does that component of your tool chest look like, and when will you commit to using it?

❑ **Your known strengths**
Your tool chest is enriched when you have clarity over your own strengths. What are they and how can you maximize their usage?

❑ **Specific focus on feelings**
Sometimes we all get caught up with our emotions and how we express them. They could be reacting to a problem that you are dealing with on your own, around an observation that you have made. There could be an issue between you and someone else. What role can emotions and feelings play in our working relationships? Why is it important to tap into feelings?

- Uncover true motivations
- Touch on beliefs and values
- Ground the conversation
- Bring you closer to the client in partnership
- Own feelings to be able to move through a block and beyond
- Help see through another lens

What happens if we ignore feelings that surface during conversation with a client? Here are some good examples to illustrate:

Feelings of frustration: "I am so frustrated. I can't believe we didn't have the winning offer!"

Feelings of sadness: "I am ever so sad to sell this home that's been in our family for decades."

Feelings of dread: "What if we can't get into the market and get priced out?"

Feelings of hope: "I just hope they accept our offer, or take our counter-offer."

Feelings of happiness: "It would be so awesome to find a home like that."

If we ignore our client's feelings, we are missing a great opportunity to genuinely engage and understand. It might or might not be costly. However, if we embrace how they are feeling, we exercise greater awareness, empathy, and understanding. We build better trust and a platform upon which to dig deeper to get to bedrock or move forward to solutions.

Being comfortable with emotional client expression is a sign that you are engaged and walking with them, rather than leading and preferring not to get drawn in.

Expression of emotions can be a brilliant cue for coaching out the why behind them and an opportunity to work together to find a resolution to the issue at hand.

❑ **Metaphors to build a clearer picture.**
It is said that a picture paints a thousand words. A metaphor is defined by Oxford Dictionaries as "a thing regarded as representative or symbolic of

something else." A simple illustration of the power of the language metaphor (or simile) can be seen in how we express how we are feeling. For example, "I feel cold" is weaker than "I am as cold as ice."

When you think about it, roadblocks can occur frequently through the regular process of dialogue. What a metaphor can do is bridge the divide and reframe the message to be conveyed. For example:

"Mary and John, I noticed during our last home tour that you were not quite on the same page in terms of your reactions and comments about the homes we viewed. Can I have your permission to slow our train down for a few moments and quietly slip off into a railway siding before we reach the point of getting derailed?"

Also, just as we promote the use of powerful questions, think the same way about metaphors. Use them sparingly but powerfully.

What does success breed?

In sports, in business, in general life, success breeds confidence. So, when you establish and define what success looks like for you, determine also what it is you will measure consistently that feeds into that feeling of confidence, irrespective of the circumstance in which you are working.

We all have a different idea of what success looks like, yet our industry tells us that we should measure it by the number of transactions we attain and volume of earnings we achieve. To some extent that holds validity, but it recognizes only one element of success: production. It is not really a fair playing field: on the surface all agents have unlimited income potential and the freedom to create whatever business they like, yet, in reality, we are all wired differently. For some, achieving top 10 percent or even top 1 percent of agents in production is super important, and that is all fine, but it means the other 90 percent of agents are not recognized for their professional contributions. Indeed, most brokerages have their own recognition programs, but still the industry norm points toward the bright lights being the producers.

When we take our examination and choose a brokerage, our motivations and objectives are not consistent. Therefore, how can we all fit into one uniform method of recognizing success?

This is where you have full rein to design what your success looks like. If it is not only about making "X" number of transactions or helping "X" number of families move successfully or making "X" amount of gross commissions, then what is it? What is in that picture of success for you? For those of you able to define the elements that compose that picture of success, I believe you will increase the likelihood of enjoying a quiet confidence.

How can you measure your success when actual sales are not happening? How else can you gain confidence and satisfaction from things you are doing well and accomplishing? What if you identify the elements that make up a meaningful work week, monitor your actions, and start to track and measure what you set out to do against what you are actually doing?

I recall a fantastic real estate agent sharing with me how she sets up her role so that she can derive benefit from working with a client, even when no sale results. She has found that such clients can be her biggest advocates and refer business to her. How is that possible? Because she does not define success as being simply sales-based.

Do you need to disarm the entitlement trap?

Think for a second about how we approach our business. Agents are protective of their contact databases, and understandably so. Some of these databases are sorted into categories depending on the perceived level of loyalty and perhaps history. However, in reality, many of these contacts know a number of agents, and how a choice is made does not always seem to make sense.

In one example, I recall a conversation recently about what we can call "calendar entitlement." A veteran agent shared a story about how they could not believe that "their" client, who had been receiving a wall calendar for years and years from them, had actually listed their property with a different agent. Indeed, how many times have you walked into an actively listed home to notice a calendar that does not match the name on the sign outside?

In another example, I was in conversation with an agent years ago who had returned from vacation to see that "his" client had listed his property with another agent in the same office. From his perspective, they had been friends for years and had had lots of conversations about real estate over that time, and the client had known he'd been in the business for years. I was curious to find out from the agent who earned the listing the *why* behind him being chosen ahead of the miffed agent. The answer was interesting, something along the lines of: "He told me that he didn't really feel that the agent was fully engaged in the business anymore."

Do you feel entitled to someone's real estate business? It can become an expectation, a tendency to feel this way as time passes and we continue to market ourselves and our services to them through newsletters, event invitations, emails, social media posts, etc. The reality, of course, is that consumers have every right to choose their professional service provider. There is no entitlement. Feeling floored because someone listed or bought with another agent is a feeling many agents have experienced, and at the time it likely evoked thoughts of self-doubt and planted seeds of uncertainty, likely putting a nice dent in confidence as a result. However, if we recognize that entitlement doesn't really make sense, what purpose does it serve to be affected in this way?

What happens if you challenge this kind of assumption and reframe thoughts of being entitled to business into earning it instead? By accepting that consumers have full choice and that we need to earn the right to do business with them, we can position ourselves more positively and act with confidence more consistently.

Have a check-in with yourself—are you setting yourself up with an attitude of entitlement? Just because someone hears from you about real estate regularly does not mean they will choose to work with you when the time comes.

Summary of core principles and self-reflection
Our learning objectives were to understand:
-   **The elements of our own professional presence**

- **How to lay a foundation of working harmoniously and effectively together**
- **How we can look at the interview process in a different way**
- **Our skills and what we have in our own tool chests**
- **The power of tapping into feelings**
- **The importance of parking thoughts of entitlement to business**

If you think about some of your behind-the-scenes norms and habits, what is surfacing?

Some questions to ponder:

Operational mode:
How would you rate your professional presence? What needs some attention?

Are you committed to developing some working guidelines with your clients?

What is in your tool chest?

How are you at building harmony with your clients?

How comfortable are you tapping into your client's feelings so that you can dig deeper and be more effective?

What are your professional fears? What specific actions can you take to minimize these fears?

Conversational mode:
How able are you to paraphrase the key points—a.k.a. golden nuggets—of a conversation?

What kind of metaphors do you use to help paint a picture?

What's behind the scenes for you?
What breeds success for you?

What action steps within your control are required to stimulate more powerful conversations and help enact meaningful change and better empowered client decisions?

Section 7

Circumstantial Confidence

Our own personal confidence—and that of our clients—is the foundation upon which we are able to make life decisions. Understanding the enablers and disablers of confidence can help us be at our most effective.

Learning objectives are to understand:
- **Some of the key situations that challenge our confidence levels**
- **How simple mindfulness techniques help prepare us to shine and be confident**
- **That a little vulnerability can be an asset**
- **The value of focusing positively on what is within our control**

This phrase, "circumstantial confidence," was born in a coaching conversation with an agent. He had mentioned having another family over to his home so that the kids could have a play date and the adults could have some good conversational time together. What followed included a less than ideal dialogue that resulted from asking directly about their friends' real estate needs. The agent reported back that it sounded awkward and completely changed the atmosphere of their afternoon conversation. He just didn't feel good about it. We then talked about how different circumstances give rise to differing levels of confidence, and this chapter was born.

To quote from *The Power of Curiosity* again, "There is no greater distance between two people than misunderstanding. Understanding others is the sweet spot in life where we learn, connect, inspire, innovate and collaborate. Our relationships are strengthened, our self-confidence is boosted, and anything becomes possible."

In the case above, the agent told me that his confidence was reduced from the conversation—he'd felt an urge to "bring up" real estate instead of understanding that this was an organic, everyday conversation between friends rather than the forcing of an opportunity. If we focus on understanding other people and take into account the perspectives that they look at life from, we actually increase our chance of doing business with—or through a referral from—them.

How do you rebound from disappointment?
"It shattered my confidence."

"I don't know how I'll be able to recover from that."

As life unfolds, we are all tested. As sure as we are alive, we'll have times when our confidence ebbs and other times when it flows beautifully (something we might loosely call "being in the zone").

Before we look at how we can rebound, we're going to take a brief look at five example situations within the real estate context, ones where our professional confidence can be tested.

Before that, take a look at the adjustment to our Partnership Framework:

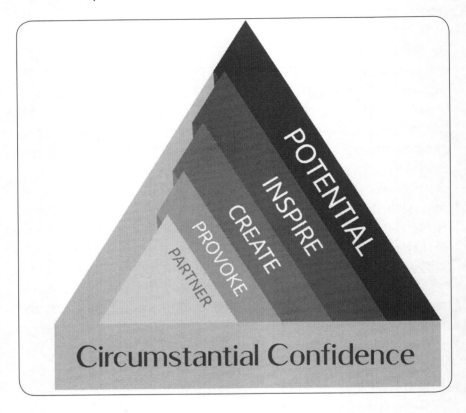

When I thought it through, it was clear that confidence is such a foundational element. That's why it props up everything else. Makes sense?

Confidence with conversations that span the career bridge

As a newer agent, how do we broach our career change in conversations and interact from a new perspective?

If you think back to those first few weeks and months as a new agent, it was a bit of an odd time, wasn't it? The peaks and valleys of each week and the uncertainty about what you should actually be spending your time doing are confidence shakers—it is a very challenging time! What are we supposed to say to people we have been friends with or known for years, worked with for years, now that we have our license and hope that there is a seller or buyer in their midst?

With the people that you know—what is often referred to as your sphere of influence—a good starting point is basic and fundamental curiosity. If you set yourself up to try to persuade and convince your friends and colleagues that they should be buying or selling, you could soon have a lot of exes. Shift your perspective and ask yourself how you react when friends are trying to sell you something. Does that sound a bit awkward to you?

Instead, replace *persuading* and *convincing* with simple, true curiosity and engage the people in your life in conversation, and see where it goes. Not pre-scripted and directive conversation that needs to automatically lead to real estate, but genuine and authentic interactions that aim purely at building on those friendships and past working relationships.

As a general rule, when you ask someone how their life is—where they have been on vacation, how their kids are, how their work is—don't you find they will generally do the same? That is simple conversation.

One thing we know: it is important to be out there meeting people and having conversations as often as possible. You could stay in a room and build the most market or product knowledge possible, you could have the most appealing website and fantastic negotiation skills, but all will be meaningless unless you have some clients.

So, can you commit yourself to *asking* instead of *telling*, to getting out of your comfort zone and reaching out to as many people as you can? You might be pleasantly surprised where a solid conversation will take you in future when you really engage your sphere of influence and gradually build upon those conversations over time. With consistency of interaction, it will likely lead to transactions with new people as well, as your sphere starts feeling comfortable and confident to refer you to them.

Conversations that commit to building partnership will generate business over time. It is that simple. It is paramount to understand what "over time" means— essentially, it's when your clients are ready and have a need to employ your services. Be clear about your intentions or you risk a lack of integrity and you might be seen as desperate for business. As someone once said to me, "People don't want you looking at them like they are a bag of groceries!" So, knowing that, it is prudent to focus on the actions rather than the results. Be eminently patient! If you are able to execute the appropriate actions regularly, over a period of time, you will greatly increase your chance to produce the results you are aiming for.

Don't push the results—develop the behaviours that will lead to the results.

How do we know this is true? Talk to the serious producers in the business. They know exactly where their business is sourced and what actions it takes to duplicate those successes, as they have performed them consistently over a long time.

Embrace the people you knew in your pre-real-estate life and calmly maintain your confidence. Do not go straight into "sales mode" with these people; be more magnetic in attracting them to your services as time moves on and their requirements activate.

Confidence with conversations for generating new clients

We have talked about the people you know—think about all the other ways you can create clients from new people you meet through your career. For example: meeting people through holding open houses or generating a meeting from a phone call. One thing is common for all methods—all these marketing channels and business-building activities we can choose to engage in all lead towards one thing: a conversation. Be genuine; be real.

In terms of lead-generating activities with people new to you, these are some of the most taxing in terms of how they can influence confidence. I remember going door-knocking for the first time at the start of my career. I left the office and drove to a neighbourhood called Point Grey. As I got out of my car, I was aware of two things: my heart was thumping and my imagination was telling me that in every house someone was observing me from an upstairs window. It felt hostile—and it was all created in my own mind.

I opened a gate, walked up a path, rang the doorbell ... and waited. And there was no one home. "Oh, thank goodness" was my reaction! *"Phew!"* Next door, same thing: no one home. The third door was answered. I said what I said, handed over a flyer and the response from the presumed homeowner was, "You guys are all the same." He let go of the flyer, which then slowly flew side to side and downwards into his recycle bin. This was followed by the door shutting firmly in my face.

I drove back to the office in silence, defeated, with shattered self-confidence and a feeling of low self-worth.

I smile as I look back on that experience (and I did successfully earn some business farming some neighbourhoods in later times). I smile because the way I set myself up for that experience was non-existent. What was I expecting? For homeowners to say, "Oh, thank goodness you're here, your timing is perfect!"? Training back then was more the "here's what you say and do" kind. After all, who was I to question that? Plus, my flyer was in colour; I thought it looked great and it was the conclusion of much careful design work.

It is valuable to be clear of your intentional outcome

What are you aiming for through a certain interaction? What is your expectation? For example, many newer agents decide on a whim to go and knock on some doors. They ask around for what to say and are essentially hoping they will knock on the door of a very pleasant homeowner who has decided they want to sell their home and are grateful the agent is there to take the listing. I am being somewhat facetious, of course, but what are many agents hoping will happen?

If the intended outcome is to promote a particular listing or sale around the corner, or to put a face to a name following some specific neighbourhood marketing, then it is easier to understand the value that is intended to be delivered by the agent.

So, for any agent who is considering embarking on a business-building activity that they have not engaged in before, where you are trying to generate leads from strangers, start by partnering with yourself first. Are you clear about your intentions and how the activity fits into the objectives of your business and your system?

Also, let's take a step back to the people who we already know. Why is it that some newer agents assume that the people they know will not give them an opportunity to do business with them? That kind of self-doubt can be limiting and remove a great potential source of clientele. Do you really want to do that? And the bigger question is: can you afford to do that? Instead, I encourage you to engage in conversations that build rapport and trust over time. As the old saying goes, you can be someone's agent before they actually need you. One part of your job is positioning yourself to be on that person's radar when the need for an agent arises, and then, based on the trust and confidence they have in you, aim to be their first choice and earn their business.

Confidence in maintaining client relationships with those in your database

Depending on which market you operate in and the legislation that an agent needs to adhere to, taking care of initial disclosure paperwork is actually just the beginning of the journey.

Take a look at the currency of your business and those relationships that are just getting in play. Think of it as a tennis match, with that first paperwork step serving to get you onto the playing surface. You're standing there, facing each other, ready to start the match. You're looking forward to the game—hopefully a match that reaches its conclusion with you walking off together as partners having enjoyed the experience and both benefitting from it. "Wasn't that great?" you might both share. The game commences with that first serve...

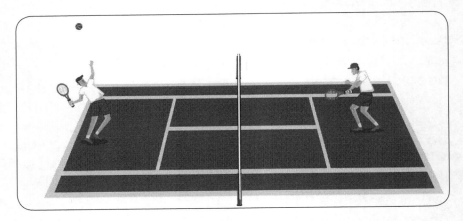

What if a racquet breaks? What if you lose all the tennis balls? What if, halfway through the match, one of you just walks off without even saying anything and you are left without your partner?

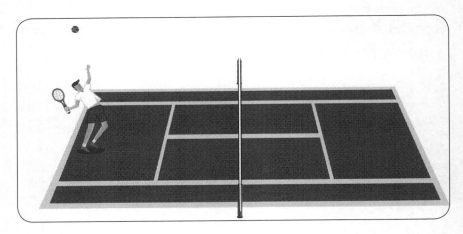

It's a bit like what can happen in real estate sales—we start out with good intentions to seeing the job through and, in many cases, it leads nowhere and we (and our ex-clients) are left unfulfilled.

Agents have databases of various sizes, living entities that are the foundation of their client base and system for business generation. They often comprise various labels that agents themselves decide upon, which help to categorize or weigh a contact in terms of motivations, interests, timelines, and so on. Many of the most productive, driven agents excel in this area and use a system that essentially drives their business. They are often clearly able to articulate how many touches recipients receive each year and what each touch intends by way of value.

From conversations over the years, I have found this to be an area that demands clarity, as it really speaks to confidence. What price do you pay for:

- not being clear about your communications plan?
- not engaging consistently with people?
- having a database that saps your confidence, as you haven't connected with some of the people in there for so very long that you wonder if they'll even remember you?

Are you proactively sowing the seeds of database-managed communication so that you can reap the rewards in the future by engaging with these people? Or are you reactively running your business oblivious to how often you even reach out to them?

Confidence comes through engagement and taking action. Confidence sinks with a deficit mindset and a dull awareness gnawing away at you for your inability to communicate effectively with those in your database. What price will you pay in the long term?

Also, think about your current clients—are you actively playing tennis with them, or is there a chance that one of you is going to end the match before it reaches its conclusion? What impact could that have on your confidence? We make a sale, our confidence runs high. We lose a client, it sinks. So what is in your control that can keep your confidence level nicely balanced?

Confidence in a potential seller or buyer appointment

Before we get to this one, let's reflect on how we feel when we are well organized, ready, and prepared. Have you experienced that positivity when you're heading for a workout and are feeling really pumped about it, giving yourself a mental slap on the back as you walk through the doors, primed for exercise? Then you open your gym bag and realize that you left your gym shoes at home. Your inner (or maybe outer) voice says, *You stupid idiot*, as the disappointment casts a shadow over what had promised to be a full-on, healthy, and active performance.

By contrast, that simple act of checking to make sure you were fully organized and prepared would have given you the green light all the way.

Similarly, when we are going to meet a homeowner for the first time and they happen to ask about the value of a home on their street that sold four months before, isn't it reasonable to expect that we would be aware of that and have that information with us, especially if the appointment has been booked in advance? I can hear a few of you say, "Well, not really, because I do a two-step listing appointment and come back again later on with that kind of information. We don't talk price during the first conversation." That may be true, and it may be a valid approach, but you get the point, I am sure. It is arming ourselves with as much knowledge and relevant information as we can so that we are able to really connect. (The side point to this is that we assume it is okay to do a two-step appointment because that is what we prefer to do—it is our operational mode of choice.)

As covered earlier, I believe the value of high-quality presentation materials is absolutely there. However, looking at the appointment from the homeowner's perspective gives you an opportunity to wonder what they might be curious about.

If we have taken the time to put together and complete our presentation materials before we knock on the homeowner's door, and we have identified neighbouring listings and sales and driven past each of them, our confidence level will naturally be that much higher.

When we meet with the potential buyer and we have materials to hand out that can add spontaneous value to the conversation, we will naturally feel more confident.

Isn't it simple to be organized, ready, and prepared? Then, when you engage in conversation and perhaps begin with my recommended "What would you like to get out of our conversation today?" you begin to establish a foundation of partnership.

Confidence in actual listing or selling transactions

When does the pressure and expectation start to ratchet up a notch or two? It can start as soon as you hear those magical words from a buyer you have been showing properties to, when they say, "Sure, let's put in an offer." Or it might emanate from a call from another agent informing you that they have an offer on one of your listings and would like to present it or send it over.

What kind of factors influence our confidence in such scenarios? Of the many possibilities, here are some examples:

- Your level of market knowledge
- Your ability to negotiate
- Your procedural knowledge
- The client(s) you are dealing with
- The agent(s) on the other end
- Urgency and timelines to adhere to
- Subjects or condition clauses
- What price will it settle at, and will your clients be happy?
- How can you minimize buyer or seller remorse?
- Your mindset and attitude that day
- What else you have on your plate at the time
- The "what if" saboteurs that enter our minds

There are so many factors that come into play. Being able to take a step back and be mindful, present and engaged is vital to how you show up and handle each element.

Confidence with after-sales care

What are the variables here? Why is it more comfortable keeping in touch with some post-completion clients rather than others, and how can we improve that?

Doesn't the mutual desire to keep in touch speak rather directly to the partnership that was established and maintained? Recently, an agent shared with us that a client had said to him, "We're really going to miss you; what are we going to do on our Thursdays now?" as they had always seen properties on that day of the week and had now bought successfully. As he shared this, he understood that he had built a client for life and an ambassador for his business. Naturally, he felt the kind of positivity that breeds confidence.

Traditional sales training includes some good system elements you can incorporate into your own system. One example is the 1/7/30 follow-up plan: calling a buyer the day after they move in, a week later, and a month later, to check in and make sure everything is in order. This is ideally shared with your buyer at the onset of the relationship (managing expectations and working guidelines). When the time comes to hand over the keys, why not ask permission to check in on the phone occasionally to make sure everything is okay? If a partnership is in place, then it is likely to be affirmative.

"Mary, just calling to see how everything is with your new apartment. How are you enjoying it?"

A week later …

"It's the end of your first week there already, can you believe it? Quick check-in to make sure everything is working fine …"

And a month later…

"Mary, you have been there a month! As promised, my final specific check-in just to make sure everything is working fine and that you're happy with everything …" Imagine how cared for that buyer will feel. Again: an ambassador for your business.

What if the fridge isn't working or there is a leak? As you read that, does your mind say, *Oh no, I wouldn't want to hear that!* Or does is say, *Great, I am really glad I called*, as you can see an excellent opportunity to extend further customer service through your own contacts or resources?

Identifying and implementing a clear follow-up system that is yours by design will help you articulate a client-for-life business strategy that underpins your system.

The mindset for this confidence tester is critical—are you genuinely there to help, or just calling hoping everything is fine?

It is similar to something we talked about in an earlier section about handling difficult questions. We have the choice to say to ourselves. *Oh no, not that question!* or we can say, *Oh, that's a good question; I can totally handle that* … One breeds doubt, the other breaks down a barrier and removes pressure, which helps you maintain your confidence.

Confidence around your peers

We tend to revere people who have accomplished something that we have not yet, don't we? That person who has run an ultra-marathon when we are still trying to finish a 10 km run, or built a log cabin with their own hands, or has achieved a level of business clientele and expertise that we can only dream of at the beginning.

Let's remember that every single person in every single business started at day #1.

Sure, some start with advantages beyond the scope of others, such as an immediate client base, deep community connections, an amazing natural personality that attracts like a powerful magnet, or a financial depth that takes away some pressure. But instead of making excuses or wondering why others have an advantage over you, what is there in your control that can propel you forward?

Sales meetings are an interesting facet of the business. Industry attendance is low—I would suspect that most brokerages only see 25 percent of their agents at sales meetings regularly. That might also be overly-generous as an average. Yet to those who make the effort, they set their minds differently by being open to learning, to hearing about market and legal and industry changes, to feel the pulse of the room and participate in the dialogues of the day. They cannot understand why the other 75 percent don't show or see the value. They take pride in making the effort and it definitely helps their knowledge base and sense of accountability. It adds some structure to their business, a non-negotiable appointment that is only missed for good reasons, such as vacation, sickness, or actively handling an offer. Familiarity with our peers promotes confidence and provides opportunity.

So why don't the other agents show? Of course, nothing is for everyone, granted. One factor can be a lack of sales—if an office highlights listing or sales successes, then some agents feel at a loss and not able to contribute, and allow themselves to suffer in silence as others in the room remain in the limelight. This consistent inaction can be detrimental to mindset, confidence, and future success, and, for some, that intentional self-exclusion puts one foot on the path toward the career exit door.

Being comfortable around your peers and genuine in your recognition of their achievements will only serve to help build your self-confidence. Can you see the benefit of applying a positive spirit of generosity over a negative spirit of exclusion?

What did Dale Carnegie (*How to Win Friends and Influence People*) have to say about this whole subject?

"Inaction breeds doubt and fear. Action breeds confidence and courage. If you want to conquer fear, do not sit home and think about it. Go out and get busy." Well said, sir.

Let's tie this in to three key values that you are able to bring to your clients as an agent:
- You can be an **expert knowledge interpreter**
- You can be an **expert negotiator**
- And if you can develop into being an **expert, curious guide**, you will stand out from the crowd.

How can you employ mindfulness to help your confidence?

Geoffrey Soloway is a mindfulness expert who I had the pleasure of meeting several years ago as part of my coach training. His "take five" approach—five long breaths to come back fully into our body—is a great way to introduce mindfulness into our business practices in a simple and easy-to-understand way. In fact, it only takes a couple of minutes to experience and realize how enabling it can be. Try it …

Sit on your chair, feet flat on the floor, hands in your lap, and close your eyes. Take a nice, slow deep breath in … hold it for three or four seconds … and let it out again. Feel your feet on the floor, the chair against your back; hear the calmness in the room … continue to breathe in and out. Then, slowly open your eyes and come back into the room.

How does that feel? It can be a wonderful way of bringing ourselves into the present in a calming and purposeful way. It's a marvellously simple version of mindfulness.

What if you are able to apply this to your day-to-day business? How do you prepare yourself for the many challenges that each day can bring? Let's identify five basic examples of professional interactions when the butterflies might start making their presence known …

- You've just arrived outside a listing appointment and look out to see this amazing potential listing. Are you thinking about the listing? Are you worrying if your pricing beliefs match those of the owner?

- You're just about to pick up a buyer to start a tour of properties. Can you keep on schedule? Will they like any of them?

- You're preparing to start the open house as the clock ticks close to the start time. Will anyone come? Do you have all the information you need?

- You are preparing to go in and present an offer. How will the seller and their agent react? Can you win the multiple offer battle?

- Before you start announcing a new listing or sale at your office sales meeting you realize it's been a while since you had the spotlight. Do you have all the facts at hand?

There are so many thoughts that can dart through your mind in these scenarios, these moments that precede what is about to unfold. Whatever you have done in the day up to that point leads to how you are feeling. Ask yourself how ready you are to take on that next task; luxuriate in that moment and give yourself permission to relax and enjoy it without pressure. How do you think this will affect how you turn up for that appointment or meeting? Easier, calmer, less pressured, focused, and ... confident.

Geoffrey Soloway taught me that this mindfulness is all about "bringing our presence and awareness into the coaching relationship." He acknowledged that, as humans, our minds tend to wander 50 percent of the time and that this type of simple technique can make a big difference in how we feel when that door opens and a business interaction begins.

Don't be shy of trying this out, even if like me you are starting out as a neophyte in this area. Practise will be beneficial, and the results of mindfulness integration will speak for themselves over time. Imagine the difference between:

-   turning up late for a listing appointment, being nervous as you allow yourself to get attached to the outcome, and becoming increasingly fearful of not earning the listing,

Versus:

-   engaging in mindfulness, being relaxed, and simply looking forward to exercising curiosity and having a great conversation.

Which do you think has the greater chance of success? Which do you believe will lead to a better mutual experience and enjoyment of that time?

Passion and positivity

What does it take for us to embrace the concept of market irrelevancy? In other words, to detach ourselves from whether it's a good, bad, or indifferent market and instead show up with a positive outlook and mindset and focus on what is in our control. This is a wonderful conversational opportunity.

How passionate are you about what you do? When we are passionate, amazing things can happen. People always have needs. Need is driven by them, not the market. Birth, death, a partnership, a marriage, a divorce, an investment—there is always need. If you focus on the market, it is the same as focusing only on price in a price-reduction conversation instead of focusing on the lifestyle impact of not taking action on price.

Find what you are really passionate about in your business and go do it! As negativity creeps in, confidence starts to wane. As positivity replaces it, confidence grows alongside it.

Is vulnerability holding you back?

Stop thinking you can't do something! What if you accept and embrace vulnerability and turn it into a strength?

So many people in sales walk around feeling deficient in terms of their business, their experience, their skillset, their foundation. How does it help to think that you need to be a certain way? Stop feeling that you have a disadvantage or are missing a piece of the puzzle, because it really doesn't help!

This is equally applicable to the brand-new agent who feels vulnerable to being asked a question they cannot answer, or an experienced agent who feels vulnerable to the speed of change in technology. Instead, what happens if you embrace your vulnerabilities?

When we are open to exhibiting some vulnerability on occasion, it is okay to acknowledge it. For example, acknowledging that you don't know a specific piece of information but offering to get it. Vulnerability shows we are real and honest, and it elicits greater confidence in your client when they really trust you for being who you are. I would wager that being open and honest is preferable to pretending and trying to be something or someone else.

So, accept yourself for who you are and ask yourself what your own inner power is, so that you can tap into it. What is your strength when it comes to engaging clients? It's okay if someone asks a question and you don't know the answer, you can always find it. Remove that kind of doubt and fear, as all it does is drain your confidence.

To me, confidence is a state of mind and a state of being. I believe we can choose to be confident—not by trying to be someone else (as the old saying goes: be yourself; everyone else is already taken), but by embracing who we are. Confidence is key to so much of what we all do, and by recognizing the impact of actions that can negatively affect it we can dramatically help ourselves perform more effectively.

Summary of core principles and self-reflection

Our learning objectives were to understand:
- **Some of the key situations that challenge our confidence levels**
- **How simple mindfulness techniques help prepare us to shine and be confident**
- **That a little vulnerability can be an asset**
- **The value of focusing positively on what is within our control**

If you reflect back over your career, whether it's a few months or maybe several decades, how confident have you been? Are you enabling yourself to reach your potential?

Some questions for you:

Operational mode:
When you think of mindset, do you hold yourself responsible for your success every day?

Your behaviours: are your daily work activities in full alignment with achieving your goals?
Self-care: how aware are you of your own wellness activities, and are there enough?

What do you see as being your role? What has changed as a result of this book?
What activity that you are passionate about gives you the greatest satisfaction?
What do you want your clients to most appreciate about you?

Conversational mode:
Can you embrace vulnerability in your conversations on occasion? How?

What's behind the scenes for you?
What makes you feel vulnerable? How can you find a solution for that?

What action steps within your control are required to stimulate more powerful conversations and help enact meaningful change and better empowered client decisions?

Are you on the way to building deeper, more effective working relationships with your clients?

Section 8

Conversations in Buyers', Sellers', and Transitioning Markets

How do changing market conditions affect the focus of our conversations?

Learning objectives are to understand:
- **Market irrelevancy**
- **Market relevancy and identifying opportunity**
- **Embracing coaching to magnify your value**
- **How fixation with price can be a distraction**
- **That our conversational approaches adjust with the markets**

Think about the laws of supply and demand and how they apply across a broad spectrum of industries. Each sector will experience transitions through different market cycles over time. Our context of real estate really is a great industry to show how some of these coaching principles can be applied to the different challenges that surface as markets transition.

We know that there is a constant need for the buying and selling of real estate, and that adopting a "market-irrelevant" stance to running your business successfully makes a ton of sense in terms of executing behaviours consistently in order to generate enough clients to reach objectives. Any seasoned real estate professional understands that markets fluctuate. It seems hard to believe, when we are full steam ahead in a strong sellers' market, that things will ever slow down. Properties sell only days or even hours of being on the Internet, snapped up through fast-paced multiple-offer scenarios, often with "subject to" clauses eliminated simply to be competitive. These markets feel insatiable and prices tend to gallop upwards with fervour. Then, sales start to slow, supply grows, and the market balances out. After that, what happens when the slowdown continues? Supply far exceeds demand, prices soften, and buyers become very reluctant to enter the market.

The question is whether any specific conversational opportunities come with these extreme fluctuations in favour of buyers and sellers.

Let's review five market phases, how they vary, and what key opportunities they present. (Note that definitions likely vary between geographic areas).

1. Finding opportunity in a slow buyers' market

– Fewer offers, lower sales volumes, subject clauses very common, greater supply, confidence to buy is lower as prices are falling, sellers resistant to dropping their prices. **Opportunity: to coach your buyers to explore buying in this slow market.**

2. Finding opportunity when transitioning toward a buyers' market

– Slowdown in offers, slowdown in sales volumes, slowing demand, subject clauses coming back in, supply starting to increase, and flattening of prices. **Opportunity: to coach your sellers about the impact of market change.**

3. Finding opportunity in a balanced market

– Balanced conditions are easy to understand in that supply and demand are in harmony. This is what we might consider a normal market with regular opportunities. Typically good sales volumes, prices steady. **Opportunity: to do everything in this book as normal procedure!**

4. Finding opportunity when transitioning towards a sellers' market

– Increase in offers, sales volumes, and demand, subject clauses start disappearing to be competitive, supply starting to get eaten up, properties selling more rapidly and prices trending upwards. **Opportunity: to coach your buyers about the impact of change.**

5. Finding opportunity in a hot sellers' market

– Multiple offers common, subject clauses often waived completely to be competitive, less supply, confidence to buy and sell is higher as prices are rising, sellers happy to sell, buyers sometimes grateful to get into the market. **Opportunity: to coach your buyers to explore coming out on top and buying in this crazy market.**

Markets are different everywhere, so the conditions listed out above are examples to illustrate some potential differences. Instead of worrying about every one being appropriate in your market, I invite you to identify and focus in on several opportunities that will be there.

In market number 5, as an agent, how do you feel when you and your buyers lose out ... again? Disappointment can move all the way through to despair, depending how often this has been happening. Your buyers say things like, "We'll never get into the market," or "Prices are crazy—we might as well give up, we can't stand it anymore!"

Then, sometime later when the market has moved through 4 to 3 to 2 and then 1, cooling right off, and you show these same buyers a property that rivals or even exceeds the quality of the one they lost out on, they are now not interested in writing an offer. Why is that? Normally, there are two factors at play: they have lost some confidence in the market, having been part of the frenzy that has now abated, and they believe prices will go even lower. Often, these buyers feel a sense of empowerment; having been victims of the previous market conditions, they are now in the driver's seat and feel there is no need to rush into any decisions until the market hits the bottom.

Every active buyer has a motivation to buy or their agent would not be in business. Yet, so many buyers in these changing markets become obsessed with the belief that prices will fall further and they can lose sight of the actual benefits that have unfolded in front of their eyes. Picture a field of sheep that slopes gently downward toward a gate. In the hot sellers' market, all of those sheep are wildly trying to barge their way through the gate, which is way too crowded to allow them all through. Yet, they are competing to make it through. In a buyers' market, those same sheep are dotted around the field. There are only one or two inquisitively looking through the gate, waiting to see if they really want to go through but unsure because others around them are hesitating.

The real estate market can be similar. In hot markets, pre-sale projects can have buyers lined up round the block, with way more buyers than there are units available. It becomes a feeding frenzy when only a select few can get through that gate. Then, when the market cools, those line-ups reduce, and confidence reduces with it. Sometimes supply can exceed demand, translating into slower sales and no upward price pressure. This results in these active buyers becoming more inactive and remaining inside that field as potential buyers.

So, let's go back to a scenario of that hot February market where Agent Bob's client Mary had lost out on a unit similar in size, detail, and quality to the one he's just shown her now in July. There are two approaches Bob could take here, amongst others.

Old-fashioned *tell*:

"So, Mary, that's a fine unit that rivals the one you lost out on in February, isn't it? Look, the market is way softer now, prices are lower, there is more selection, you have more time to make a decision, there's less competition so we can negotiate the price, we can even have some subjects to protect you. Mortgage rates are still low. So what are you waiting for? Let's make an offer!"

In this typical *tell* approach, Bob is using his powers of *convincing* and *persuading* Mary about the benefits of a slower market. These are his solutions, and are being *presented* and *told* to her. What if he were to take a different approach?

Modern *ask*:

"So, Mary, from your perspective, how does the home we've just seen rival the one we lost out on in February?"

"Well, I would say it is very similar, perhaps even a bit better."

"How are you feeling about making an offer?"

"Hmm ... I am not sure. The market seems to have changed and I wonder if prices will drop further later this year. I don't want to pay too much."

"Thanks for sharing that. Prices may or may not be a bit lower later this year; we cannot predict the future. Actually, there is something I am really curious about. Let me take you back to that evening in February when we lost out on that similar unit which sold under multiple offers for $35,000 over the asking price. [And here's the golden question:] How did you feel that night?"

"Urghh. I felt so disappointed. Again."

"How did you *really* feel?"

"I felt like giving up. Despondent. A feeling I would *never* get into the market!"

"So, I am curious—what do you see has changed since those market conditions we had back then?"

"Well, thankfully, it looks like the market has slowed down, prices have come off a bit, there seems to be more on the market than before."

"Yes, indeed, I would agree with those three changes, for sure. What else has changed?"

"I am not feeling rushed like before! I guess it is not necessary to go in subject-free these days?"

"You are quite right. What you have listed out are some of the actual benefits to buyers like you in today's market. What possibilities do you think there could be in terms of being able to negotiate the asking price compared to back then?"

"This unit is already asking $40,000 less than that one went for, right? Do you think we could get it for even less?"

"Before we get to that, you mentioned prices could fall further. I am curious—how would we know when the market has bottomed out?"

"I am not sure. I guess when we see buyers moving back into the market in numbers and competing for properties?"

"That sounds about right to me. It is that sheep example again. People seem willing to compete when they know others want something, usually translating into a higher price. So, yes, we can certainly try our very best to negotiate the price. You are a first-time buyer and the benefits you listed out give us a better opportunity than before to get into the market, right? In February you felt you would *never* be able to. Reflecting on this opportunity, what would you like to offer?"

In these two examples, can you see the difference in telling the client what *you* think they should do versus coaching them to reach a well-thought-out client-generated solution? When you are able to inspire by aligning a client's heart and mind, you increase your chances of guiding a buyer from the fence and into the type of home that they were happy to buy in competition before at a higher price. The key here is to name the feelings—as the saying goes: "name it to tame it."

Let's play this one out in terms of retiring home sellers whose listing has been on the market for several months and they are reluctant to reduce their asking price, as they had set their expectations on achieving a certain price. Their goal is to move to the Okanagan because they love to ride their bikes, enjoy the vineyards, ski in winter and boat in summer. As well, their daughter and young family live there. The market has softened, and they just can't seem to sell. They know there are lots of great properties to choose from in that market.

They are priced at, let's say, $1,099,000. The market is soft and in October already. They have their hearts set on selling for at least $1,000,000. A similar home on their street sold last year for $1,100,000 and only last week another very similar home went for $975,000.

If you go in there and tell them they need to reduce their price, talk only about the market, and price is all you focus in on, then it is a rather one-dimensional conversation that has a lower chance of the client be able to comply with your recommendation. "Well, sorry, but we're just not interested in reducing. I guess the Okanagan can wait."

Approaching it from a coaching perspective, it might go something like this:

"Mary and George, thanks for meeting with me today. As we touched on in our phone call, your neighbour's home sold last week for quite a bit lower than we are asking—I am curious what you've been thinking about that?"

"Oh, we think they gave it away! I mean, I know old Jim was moving to the Island to be close to his grandkids, but why didn't he hold out for more?"

"I can appreciate you asking that. Why do you think he decided to accept that offer?"

"Actually, Mary bumped into him yesterday and he seems happy enough. I guess he wants to move on with his life."

"If we reflect on your reasons for putting your house up for sale, Mary, George, where are we in terms of your own life plans?"

"Hmm, on hold? It doesn't look like we'll be selling anytime soon. Pity—would have loved to have this place sold and be safe in the knowledge of spring in the Okanagan ..."

"What do you believe is holding us back from you making that a reality?"

"The market? Seems there are not many buyers around compared to when we first listed."

"What do you believe determines how much a home sells for?"

"How much someone wants to pay … and of course how much someone wants to accept."

"Thanks for sharing that, Mary. I am really curious about one thing: what impact will it have on you both—and your daughter and family—if your home stays for sale and we are unable to find a buyer?"

"More long trips up the Coquihalla Highway. Our daughter won't drive it in the cold weather, and we're not too keen, either! So I guess we won't be seeing much of them, unless we can sell soon."

"I remember earlier on you sharing with me your love of riding to the vineyards and relaxing on the water in summer with your daughter and your grandchildren. On a scale of one to ten, how important is it for you to be living there by spring and ready to live that summer dream?"

"I'm a ten; how about you, George?"

"Yep, sure would be nice."

"So what steps do you believe we need to take to bring that vision to life?"

"I guess we have to get this place sold."

"So, I am hearing from you both that reaching your original goal of selling and moving to the Okanagan is as important as ever. Can I invite you to look at things here from a buyer's perspective? If you were them, and you were looking at your listing at the price we're at and the sale down the road at that price, what would you be thinking?"

"I'd wonder what the difference is between the two, for sure."

"And, as a buyer, when you think about that difference, how do you feel?"

"I guess I might wonder if I could buy this place for that price?"

The conversation would continue on, with the agent patiently helping the clients to understand the full impact potential of price inaction and ultimately reach a conclusion.

In cases where homes are not selling and the onset of a cold winter is nigh, it is easy for a seller's mind to drift to the spring, and its offer of a greater potential to sell. In some ways, spring is the enemy. It is easy to think that conditions will be better, with bulbs starting to grow through and bring their beautiful flowers to the world, the birds happily chirping away. The assumption they are making is that the market will surely be more positive as well.

The key is to spend good time helping your client see from a 360-degree perspective and build an awareness of all possible scenarios and their impacts.

Fixation with price

Most buyers of new cars make their buying decision with the knowledge and expectation that the vehicle will typically start depreciating in value as soon as they drive it off the lot. Why would they do that? Let's say someone is buying a $50,000 vehicle that then drops to $40,000 in a very short space of time—why would they do that? Likely because (a) they love the vehicle, (b) they are not planning on selling it for many years, and (c) it is a lifestyle decision. They could buy virtually the same vehicle for less—as being pre-owned—but they happily decide for their own reasons to buy new and that's important to them.

As real estate agents, do we give enough thought to how we set out our pricing conversations? We established earlier that a price reduction conversation is not just about price; if lifestyle objectives and drivers become a focus of conversation, then we, agent and client, can mutually assess the potential impact of decisions that are made with respect to lowering the price, keeping it as is, or even increasing it. This provides a valuable backdrop upon which clients can make a price-adjusting decision instead of letting it be all about comparable listings and sales. Doesn't that make sense?

Before we get down to the final stage of making an offer or signing a listing contract, let's consider why we get so fixated on diving quickly into a price-driven conversation.

So, when you have followed the process outlined above and your client has been able to generate their own realizations about the benefits of buying in the slower market, the lifestyle conversation aligns beautifully. Our objective is to genuinely and authentically help our clients make decisions that will positively impact them, and for many, price is not the major factor.

I suggest you don't get caught up in the "yes, but" debate of buyers of cars expecting that they will depreciate versus buyers of real estate expecting it to appreciate. While being true, the real story is that lifestyle considerations outweigh financial. The financial services industry also provides clues about market timing—with many of us making regular or monthly contributions to unit trusts or mutual funds expressly so that we can smooth out the peaks and valleys of the market instead of waiting for that perfect moment.

The other piece of the puzzle is the "once the market has bottomed, I'll be buying" talk. Does that make sense? Absolutely. Who wouldn't want to buy at the bottom of the market? That line-up would go round the block again and again. However, aren't these clients making an assumption that they will even be able to?

When markets bottom, we only find out later. An article appears maybe a month or two after—or longer—with an expert commentator pulling out when it actually happened from statistics. What can then follow is a sudden resumption of buying activity and prices start to rise accordingly. So, those buyers who have been patiently waiting are now back out there in competition with each other, with less if any room to negotiate, apply conditions, have time to make a decision, etc.

So, ask yourself: what price do we pay if we allow ourselves, as agent and client, to make price the sole focus of conversation? We can really miss a wonderful opportunity to help our clients make a change that impacts their lives.

What about the transitioning markets?

As markets slow, there can be a period when sellers take time to adjust, and find it challenging. Conversely, as markets pick up, buyers are challenged by the new forces of competition and pressure. In both cases, agents can add substantial value by coaching their clients to think through the impact of these changes upon their lifestyle or investment goals. Making a decision can sometimes feel like the hardest thing to do—in hot markets, how much over the asking price as a buyer should you offer? In slow markets, how much lower than your asking price should you be willing to accept?

In both hot and cold scenarios, you will serve your clients best by engaging them in the actual processes around their decisions. In other words: what price for inaction or poor decisions?

For those buyers, great thought-provoking questions might be:

"When you wake up in the morning and realize that you have been successful, at what price will you be comfortable with your decision?"

"What if I came back here this evening to let you know that someone else offered $10,000 higher than you—would you have wished that you had offered more? Or would you be comfortable in letting it go?"

Summary of core principles and self-reflection
Our learning objectives were to understand:
- **Market irrelevancy**
- **Market relevancy and identifying opportunity**
- **Embracing coaching to magnify your value**
- **How fixation with price can be a distraction**
- **That our conversational approaches adjust with the markets**

How many of these markets have you been involved in?

Questions to ask yourself:

Operational mode:
What is your track record in being able to articulate taking action with buyers and sellers? And what is the potential impact of not being able to do so?

When encouraging a client to make change, is your strategy to focus predominantly on lifestyle or price?

Conversational mode:
How valuable have your conversations been with your buyers and sellers concerning the impact of changing market conditions?

How successful have you been in coaching sellers around price in declining markets?   .

How successful have you been in coaching your buyers to move off the fence and make a positive decision?

What's behind the scenes for you?
Are you able to take on board the learnings of this section?

What needs addressing in how you handle market conversations?

What action steps within your control are required to stimulate more powerful conversations and help enact meaningful change and better empowered client decisions?

Section 9

Skills development that will advance you ahead of the crowd

Essential skills that will enable you to outperform others on the playing field, and, most importantly, increase value for your clients.

Learning objectives are to understand:
-   **The skills that provide an exciting growth edge for you as a real estate professional**
-   **How to build the bridge between *asking* to *advising***
-   **The power of providing positive feedback for questions**
-   **How important silence can be in creating thinking space**
-   **Heading to source before solution**
-   **What active listening really is and the power of great questions**
-   **Exciting new visualization techniques for your clients**

Sensing versus thinking

As you build better coaching proficiencies, you will go from *thinking* to *sensing*. This is what allows the thinking to happen differently and it will help you be creative and ask some deeper, more thought-provoking questions.

"There is something I am sensing from what you have shared with me ..." really engages and builds partnership. *Sensing* happens as you are able to relax and feel the pulse of a conversation. It is sometimes being able to sense what is not being said—anything from the elephant in the room to the subtlest of nuances—as well as finding a golden nugget that will help propel the conversation forward and more deeply for mutual benefit.

Another valuable part of the client-centred approach is enhancing and developing the trusted relationship by prompting language *around* the senses: "what I am hearing, how do you feel about that, what are your thoughts, what are you seeing?" Simple language but extremely impactful for clients who are having difficulty making a listing, selling, or buying decision.

I also find that the words "sensing" and "curious" have special qualities to them, if used skillfully. For example, if someone says to you, "I am really curious about something," or "there is something here that I am sensing," don't you feel immediately drawn-in and focused to hear what will follow?

So, see if you can bring this skill into your conversations—you'll see a difference!

Asking to *advising*—the transitional bridge

If you believe in the pure power of *asking*, then it is equally important to recognize another art form to master: how and when to transition the conversation from *asking* mode to mentoring and actually providing some ideas and solutions. "A-ha," I can hear you say. "We can't just sit there asking a bunch of questions all day!" Patience, now ...

Very true. You cannot. However, be acutely aware that when you have been nicely engaged in a pure coaching conversation (that is, no *telling*, lots of *asking*, drawing solutions out of the client) and you say something like, "Okay, let me tell you why I think this makes most sense," you are suddenly closing off the whole free flow and dynamic of the conversation.

I remember this happening in one of my sessions, while in a role-play with an agent who had assumed the role of a seller. This particular seller didn't want to reduce their asking price, being that it was November, and instead was thinking of listing his property again the following spring as he felt the market could be stronger. I played the agent's role and, as the conversation was gaining depth and value and we were really exploring motives, fears, expectations, and so on, I purposefully and suddenly added in: "But I want to caution you—what if the market is not higher in the spring, then what?"

As we debriefed, both he and others in the class shared how that one *telling* input from me completely changed the whole dynamic and feel of the conversation in a negative way, as I had, in effect, stifled the oxygen to his own internal thinking. The real effect of that one statement I made was to put us figuratively back on opposite sides of the table instead of authentically working together as a team, as partners.

This transitional part of the conversation is highly interesting to me, and the best suggestion I have around this is to either use your own gut feeling as to when the time is right or, better still, check in with your client. It definitely takes some real awareness and presence to handle to best effect. Think about it: we have been standing together with our client as partners engaged in conversation and drawing lots of interesting thoughts and ideas out. Ahead of us both is a bridge that leads us forward as we make a transition from *asking* to *advising*. The best-case scenario is that we take this journey together. Conversely, the worst-case scenario is that you leave your client on this side of the bridge as you make the crossing.

What could cause that detachment? It could be that there is still unfinished business in terms of things that haven't been covered or discussed enough. It could be that the client is still curious about something or needs further assistance in working through an issue that's on their mind. Your mutual objective, if indeed you are a good fit to be working together, is to cross that bridge as working partners.

You will be best served in making a great transition from *asking* to *advising* when you have a keen awareness of both the conversational contract (what your client stated they wanted to actually get out of the conversation) and, as importantly, where you are in the dialogue. It is also very valuable to acknowledge the transition with some words that seek permission to advise.

There are clues that will be present to help determine this timing, like when the conversation has gone very well, as indicated by your client in their direct feedback.

To do a proper transition and add that transitional bridge to the conversation, try something like:

"Mary, can I check in with you—have you taken what you need from our conversation in terms of being crystal clear about your buying objectives?"

"Matt, yes, thank you. You have been awesome; you've really helped me focus."

"Excellent. I am sensing that we work well together. So are you ready now to move our conversation into the listing documentation and get your home on the market?" [In other words, are you ready to cross the bridge with me?]

"Yes, I think I'm comfortable to list with you."

At this point, most of what you do is in that mentoring role as the licensed professional.

There's a great example in section 8 that highlights how to coach a seller by focusing less on price and more on lifestyle.

In terms of the transition from *asking* to *advising*, once a client has generated a price or a choice solution, then you are able to provide perspectives, opinions, and professional advice—mentoring, in a sense—and there is definitely a healthy co-existence of coaching and mentoring that helps your real estate buyers and sellers to make the best decisions.

By drawing out from them first, not only are you empowering your clients, you are also setting up the perfect space to share your high-value professional advice. And yes, there is plenty of time for that!

Also, here are three "i" words that have surfaced in class which really speak to the essence of approaching things in an authentic, natural way, and serve as a guide to making the transition:

Instinct – "Trust your instincts" is something we hear or say. Like gut feeling, it speaks to a naturalness of our reactions or impulses to take a certain action. As the conversation starts to offer up opportunity to make a transition from asking to advising, listen to your instincts—what are they saying to you? Often, they can be a valuable internal guide.

Intuition – Similarly, our intuition can be a guide for us. What is that inner voice or sense silently saying to us? Is it right more than it's wrong for you?

Introspection – Examining what lies within us as people; reflecting from the inside out. The more we are able to achieve this for ourselves as agents, the more we can help ourselves develop clarity of purpose. Also, the more we can encourage this in terms of client self-discovery, the more we can raise the potential of client-generated solutions.

Positive acknowledgement and handling tougher questions

Sometimes, conversations can be challenging. A good example of this is when someone asks for a discount. As an example, the recipient of the question could be an artist who has toiled for hours on a painting, a cabinet maker who has created an intricate piece of furniture, a stockbroker, a financial advisor or a real estate agent who is proposing a fee for the services they are hoping to provide.

What do all of these scenarios have in common? A potential buyer of the goods or service asking for a lower price. And why shouldn't they?

With commissions, often people want to be heard in terms of what they see you are earning. It is reasonable to ask such questions and invites a dialogue between agent and client.

How do we react to such questions? Do we immediately think, *Oh no, not* that *question, that's all I need!* and then, by default, go into defensive mode? If we think back to traditional training, it falls into the "handling objections" category and, among a number of canned responses, one approach can include a simple statement such as:

"Would you reduce your fee for me?"

"No. Any other questions?"

Reflect on the quality of that answer. While it may work for some agents, doesn't it sound a bit like the antithesis of partnership?

How could that be handled differently? What if you are immediately able to think, *Ah, great, I welcome that question.* So, instead of immediately declining the request, you actually welcome the question and start with a nice acknowledgement of it instead, something like:

"Thanks for bringing that up, I appreciate your question. I am curious to find out why that might be important to you?"

Remember, sometimes a client's motive is to be heard and, in some cases, to feel they are being handled as "special clients." It is not necessarily about the money itself. A probing partnership statement to that might be:

"It sounds like you're looking for additional value—let's find other ways to get you that, shall we?" and adjust the focus to inclusions. Or, it might be:

"Thank for bringing that up; I appreciate your question. I have something here that actually breaks down what happens to the professional fees that you pay, so shall we take a look at that?"

This is a good example of what we touched on earlier: spontaneous presentation. It will serve you well to remember that your spontaneous presentation materials support you, you don't support the presentation.

I recall a time when I was giving a class to a group of a dozen agents. It was pointed out to me in that class that my questions were open-ended and vague, and I found that lovely to hear! I took it as a positive acknowledgement. Why? By allowing the client to think widely and by providing some looser interpretive space for them to reflect in, it allows me to ask a really refined and focused question—a powerful question.

In the traditional scenario of objection-handling techniques and scripts, a smug salesman is proud that he or she can handle any objection thrown at them. Like the stall objection: "Ah ... I have to check with my wife." Is this essentially a top-down approach aimed at closing a sale? I'll let you figure that one out. Is how the customer feels or how they want to be treated less important than making the sale and closing the deal? When fees are at stake, the persuading, convincing, and closing approach can be enticing. But how does the client feel? How important is that to you?

What happens when we ask, engage, and collaborate? We maintain curiosity and communicate through an instinctive conversation that can create a strong bond with a client and help them discover and be clear about what they hope to actually achieve.

As those tough questions surface, we might be able to draw upon a key resource from our presentation package that helps to further inform the conversation. When we present this spontaneously and in alignment with the present conversation, it plays a valuable back-up role to our conversation.

Another great value to your conversations that uses positive acknowledgement can be gained in how you react to a client's suggested ideal. For example, you have completed a comparative market analysis and the property clearly falls within a range of $850,000–$880,000 based on several very similar properties selling within that range. Out of the blue, the seller says to you:

"I would like to list at $995,000."

What happens to us as agents when we hear these words? How do we react, both in our own minds and verbally to the seller? One example might be:

"$995,000? That's way too high! I cannot see your property selling if you list it for that much."

Another response might be:

"Okay, so as we start looking at listing price options, we can certainly consider listing at $995,000. Pricing is actually a key part of the marketing strategy, so let's look at it in that context, shall we? Before we look at other options, I am curious ... where does that figure come from?"

In the first example, the agent has dismissed the client's suggestion as unworkable. Yes, clearly their price is too high, but by going on the offensive, the agent is putting a brick in a wall between them and their seller. Conversely, the second example positively acknowledges the seller's suggestion as an option among others that they, together, can explore. This is way more partnership-oriented and collaborative; it is non-judgemental and inclusive.

If we do a superb job of coaching around their objectives and also mentoring on strategy and advice, that combination becomes high-value and is likely to resonate and result in a good mutual decision. Conclusively, our clients are free to make whatever pricing decision they like, and then we can decide if we wish to take the business.

Delivery considerations

I remember flying back to Vancouver from Kelowna in BC's Interior on a cramped flight in one of those smaller planes. It was actually quite cool to have a window seat, as I had a bird's-eye view of the landing gear. It was quite a slim plane with jet propeller engines and one set of landing gear under each wing.

As the plane descended toward the Vancouver runway, I was fascinated to see how one strut reacted to the pressures that were being thrust upon it, moment to moment. Sure enough, a somewhat immediate hydraulic dampening ensured a beautifully smooth landing. That one piece of equipment located under each wing worked perfectly.

We all know how important that smooth landing is—particularly when we have endured one that has been anything but—so how do we land elements of our conversations as successfully? Especially when we know that the verbal component of conversation is perhaps only 7 percent of the overall communication? I believe a big part of landing a smooth and high-value conversation lies in understanding what constitutes professional presence.

Silence and space: turning awkwardness into thought-provocation

They say that silence is golden. And I am here to share with you that it is. When there is a period of silence during a conversation, most people feel awkward. This is something media interviewers thrive on—leaving an interviewee's response hanging in silence until they're compelled to fill the void with more language. Sometimes that yields the golden nuggets that make the headlines.

Silence is something to embrace. It is the gateway to deeper thinking and words percolating up from wonderful, thought-provoking questions.

So ... what if you release yourself from the urge to break the silence?

A powerful question is asked (often, simple language that shoots right to the heart of an issue). A few seconds go by, and you hear the words: "That's a great question ... I am not really sure ..." The seconds tick by. No one is saying anything. The agent then asks another question and the silence is over, and a potential moment of magic is lost.

Versus:

A powerful question is asked. A few seconds go by, and you hear the words: "That's a great question ... I am not really sure ..." The seconds tick by. No one is saying anything. The agent quietly sits, perhaps looking at his notepad, giving time for his client to really think, review, and start formulating their next thought.

Which is more powerful for both of you? The second one, of course.

Silence provides extremely valuable mental space for your client to absorb, reflect, dig deep, and respond.

Consider a scenario where a seller is fixated on listing their home at a higher price than the comparative market analysis shows is reasonable. The agent asks the client:

"Yes, we can list the property at that higher level, that is an option. But I am curious—what impact could that have on your plan of relocating to be close to your daughter and family before winter sets in and makes that journey so difficult?"

"Hmm. Well, I don't really worry about that. I can wait."

Silence.

"Well, as long as I move well before Christmas. I mean, it would be great to move in before the roads get trickier."

Silence.

"Probably end of October."

"Okay, so I am hearing that you'd like to move out by the end of October at the latest. We are in mid-July now. Typically, we have a couple of months between the sale and the move. Working backwards, how long does that give us to sell this property?"

"I guess not long. Six weeks?"

"If you were a buyer in today's market and you had all these choices, what price would make you want to come and take a look?"

And so on. Give your clients space to think! Give yourself permission to zip it up and wait it out. It is not sales gimmickry; at the right time, it can provide a breakthrough in thinking that a client needs to move forward and make a decision that is the difference between selling and not selling.

Head to the source of your client's goals, not the solution!

By now you should be well aware of the reasons we don't just want to dive straight into a solution-based conversation. The easiest example to illustrate this is with a buyer. They want to buy a home. Does your mind immediately ask, *What type? Where? What price?* etc. Or, does it immediately question, *Why?* By default, do you head straight up on the Elevator Ride? Or do you head the other way first?

Solution or source? Remember that one.

When two people sit down in conversation and one is a specialist in a certain area of interest to the other, think about preconceptions that might exist in the mind of the other person. For example: an agent meets a prospective buyer for the first time who has been referred to them by a mutual friend. The agent turns up energized and up for an engaging conversation—but how do they know if the buyer is equally positive or internally harbouring some skepticism or doubt about working with a real estate agent?

My lifelong favourite football team is Oxford United. They used to play at the Manor Ground, which was known by opposing teams to be a tough place to play because the pitch actually sloped about ten feet in elevation from one end to the other. The home team usually attacked towards our fervent home supporters in the second half, meaning that the visitors were kicking uphill for the second half of the game.

What happens when we level the playing field? Gone is the mental advantage or disadvantage one has over the other and more equitable conditions exist. Let's say this buyer has worked with a different agent before, and for whatever reason they did not have a good experience. How important is it for you as the current agent to discover exactly what that buyer is looking for from their agent? Is it equally as important as it is for you as the agent to discover if this buyer meets your definition of a great client to work with?

For example, you ask, "I understand you were working with another agent before and that it wasn't working out—I am curious, what are you looking for from me in terms of service, if we decide to work together?"

"Well, to be honest, I was working with an agent who promised me they'd work hard to help me find the right home, but they just didn't communicate well. They put me on that automatic email thing that sent me lots of listings, but rarely called to follow up or recommend any to go and see. So I feel like I have been doing the searching on my own."

"Thanks for sharing that. What for you would be most helpful for us to talk about first?" and so on.

It is important to uncover anything that might hold a client back. It seems the real estate industry is always in the spotlight, and real estate is such a popular topic, that what comes along with that is certain perceptions and misgivings. By getting those out into the open, we are increasing our chances of being able to create a strong working partnership.

The examples above are focused on the source, the underlying factors and thinking that affect decisions people make. If solutions are the roof of a house, the source is the foundation. Do a solid job in building the foundation and the roof will come in time. Do a weak job at the source and the roof may never exist. It is collaborative conversation that brings it all together and maximizes the chance of the roof fitting perfectly.

Listening choices

The clarity of the road ahead in producing solutions is determined by the quality and focus of your ability to listen. Most people, when asked, consider themselves to be good listeners, generally speaking.

In group coaching sessions, I have found a great way to find out who is present and listening actively. While the group is coaching one member around a certain topic and the conversation is unfolding, I love to pause on occasion and challenge the group to play back a key word that was shared minutes earlier. Sometimes, a door that is seen as being opened wide by a professional coach is missed by the competency learners. Other times, someone might just nail it. That shows me who is truly present and listening acutely.

Being a good listener, though, is not enough. We will give ourselves and our clients the best possible chance to reach potential by becoming really good—or hopefully even great—listeners.

What happens when we listen to understand rather than to respond?

As mentioned in section 2, a book I cannot recommend highly enough is *The Power of Curiosity* by Kathy Taberner and Kirsten Taberner Siggins. In it, they delve into what they call "The Five Power of Curiosity Listening Choices." These are:

1. **Ignore the speaker** – not listening; closed minded
2. **Focus on me** – paying attention but from my perspective; judgemental
3. **Focus on you** – paying attention, but on what they should do

4. **Focus on understanding** – actively listening, curious, open and non-judgemental
5. **Focus on us** – actively listening, curious, open and non-judgemental, with a vested interest in the outcome.

Choice number 1 is obviously tuning out what you are hearing, ignoring what is actually being said.

Choice number 2 is one that many agents make without realizing, one where they consider what is being said from their own viewpoint. This choice is focused on themselves rather than their client.

Choice number 3 is another listening choice many agents make, as it enables them to dispense advice as if the question "what would you do?" has been asked. "Well, if I were in your shoes I would …" which really makes little or no attempt to actually *understand* the speaker. This is very limitational for obvious reasons.

Choice number 4 is where we want to be as agents: committed to engaging and collaborating with clients. Your natural curiosity is aroused, and you are listening with openness and empathy, and without judgement or blame. Perfect! Use this when exploring with your client and truly finding out what they want.

Choice number 5 is equally as effective for us as agents, but plays a different role: creating or identifying common ground, speaking to working together and partnering, contemplating the "we" word as you listen with curiosity. This is also perfect within our realm of the Partnership Framework. In essence, this choice is where we move things forward to sealing the deal together.

So, I really encourage you to reflect on these five different choices for listening to a client or colleague. Great stuff, isn't it?

I remember many years ago a confident young man coming in to speak with me about potentially joining our brokerage. Answering my question about why he thought real estate sales was a good career choice for him to be making, he said, "It's an ideal business for me, because people say I'm a great talker." *Really?* In today's world of sales, is the mile-a-minute talker what the real estate—or any—consumer is looking for? I wonder: has the time of the fast-talking salesman passed?"

As I mentioned, the majority of people consider themselves to be good listeners, when asked. A good way to test this is to pair up and have one of you relate a story to the other for about two to three minutes about something significant that has happened in your life, why it happened, and the effect it has had. Then, ask the listener to paraphrase it back—in short order, summarizing the key points of what they heard. You'll likely be surprised to see how focused you had to be as the listener and how challenged you were to remember all the key points presented.

You could make a case that asking powerful questions and exercising active listening are two of the most important competencies for any consumer-serving professionals to build and maintain.

Think about how we feel when someone has taken the time and given true unbridled focus in listening to our concerns. Consider how you felt when you shared a very personal conversation about one of your life's problems with a close friend. Think about how you felt as a result of their listening and their input, and the feeling created from being able to safely unpack that problem and get it out in the open to encourage and invite perspective.

Active listening gives us the gift of being able to formulate powerful questions, and we are rewarded when (a) we hear our client say, "That's a great question," and (b) when we can see the impact it is having on moving you and your client forward together as partners in the conversation. Sometimes driving forward, sometimes driving deeper, sometimes visually imagining into the future … but without careful, acute listening we miss those conversational doors that fling open and opportunities to create more expansive, valuable dialogue.

And remember: active listening is aimed at determining what the text of the conversation is, as well as the subtext. This means being able to hear and identify not only what is being said, but also what is not being said.

Don't fall into the old trap of overcoming objections or concerns by simply trying to *convince* … there is another way that is better suited to building that partnering foundation: choosing to listen and understand, then ask great questions. *Selling, telling, convincing, persuading* are yesterday's methods—active listening and powerful questions are today's.

And while we are on the subject, here's my take: questions are crucial, but listening is critical.

Powerful questions

Unless you have no one to interact with, it is pretty much impossible to go through a day without asking a number of questions. It is as natural as breathing and starts from the tender age at which we first speak. We touched earlier on the innate curiosity that every child possesses and how in adult life we can become less curious as we become more knowledgeable. Then we become an expert in something and start to regress into a less curious state of being, using that knowledge base to *tell* and *advise* rather than being deeply curious. Why is that? My opinion is that we make a simple assumption that the person requiring or requesting our services expects us to *tell* and *advise*, and so that's what we do. And, while this is absolutely correct, it is only part of the picture.

When we consider the listening choices that we can make, we can surely see that some agents in our business ask a question and then listen to seize an opportunity to talk about themselves. They miss the actual opportunity that is opening up.

That traditional question of "what criteria do you look for in a real estate agent" illustrates this perfectly. The agent is listening to find out how they can justify being that choice by matching up with the criteria. A prospective seller says,

"Integrity is very important to me."

The agent replies, "Me too. What other criteria?"

Seller says, "Someone who is experienced."

The agent replies, "Yes, that's very important; I have nine years of experience. What else?" and so it goes on.

An agent who resists *telling* and focuses instead on building partnership would approach it very differently. For example: a prospective seller says,

"Integrity is very important to me."

The agent replies, "What is it about integrity that is important to you?"

The seller says, "Well, when someone says they are going to do something, then they do it. My last agent promised me this great long marketing plan and, frankly, they failed to deliver on much of it. I found that really disappointing."

The agent replies, "Thanks for sharing that. I can sense that meeting expectations is very important to you. It is to me, too. I am curious—what elements are you most hoping to see in a marketing plan for your home?"

Isn't it easy to see the difference? In the second example, the agent is listening to *understand*. When that agent heard the word "integrity," a pathway spontaneously opened in their mind to explore and really understand what is behind this value. It is a far cry from an agent asking for a list of criteria and then justifying why they should be "the Chosen One." As a consumer, I know which of those two choices I would prefer.

In archery, the target has a series of concentric rings. Arrows that land in the outer rings score a lesser value than those that land right in the centre. When at first we are hitting the low numbers and even some zeros, how do we feel? We're not lined up quite right, we're off-base, not focused in enough. We might feel disappointed and a bit disjointed. Compare that to when we hit the high numbers. Suddenly the world is good again, we take comfort and confidence in our ability to perform, we start to enjoy it.

Think of the variety of questions you will be asking as a quiver full of arrows, each with a sharp tip and holding an opportunity to help you score highly and engage superbly with your client. Challenge yourself to hit a few "that's a great question" bulls-eyes!

I have listened to many agents practise coaching each other and, in terms of the questions being asked, two things often stand out quite early on:

1. There is a large quantity of questions delivered in somewhat linear fashion. By that, I mean a question is asked, followed closely by another … and another … and another.

One of the skills to develop is to slow it down and land a question. We all love it when our question is met with "now that's a great question!" That is evidence of what we call a "powerful question." So be careful not to go into question overload and be aware of your rate of questions and your tone.

2. Relevancy is the second thing I notice—or lack thereof. It is one thing to ask a list of decent questions and it is quite another to ask questions which link together nicely.

Think back to the Elevator Ride—we are constantly dipping down into P1 and P2 to find out what the motivator or driving force behind something is. So ask a question, and, depending what it is, see if you can identify a really good follow-up.

As you practise your skills, ask questions to find out what the client wants and what needs to happen for them to get there. If problems, barriers, or blocks are identified, ask questions to find out what needs to happen to overcome them. Remember to recontract—remind both of you what the client wanted to get out of the conversation, reclarify anything that needs it, and enjoy the ride from P2 all the way up.

Be careful as you ask a series of questions, as you want to show up with curiosity rather than run an interrogation.

In service to helping you understand the benefit of linking questions, below is a summary of some target competency areas and clear objectives for each, plus two sets of example questions and follow-ups. They are not perfect, as there is not really a specific scenario to apply to them, but you'll see how they go quite nicely together:

Competency area: Collaboration/accountability
Objective: Determine a clear focus and a desired outcome

Example question: What would you like to get out of our conversation today?
Follow-up example: Why is that important to you?

Example question: What do you need from me to help you reach your objectives?
Follow-up example: What would be most helpful to you for us to talk about first?

Competency area: Awareness
Objective: Refine understanding of client's ability and readiness to change

Example question: What are your expectations in terms of selling this property?
Follow-up example: What else is there that I need to be aware of?

Example question: What are you hoping for in your next home?
Follow-up example: Can you share with me where this vision comes from?

Competency area: Responsibility
Objective: Helping determine a client's ability to respond with an action

Example question: Where would you assess your motivation to move, on a scale of one to ten?
Follow-up example: What would it take for that to be a nine or a ten?

Example question: Are there any challenges that you can see holding you back?
Follow-up example: Can you share with me more about that?

Competency area: Commitment
Objective: Align with client actions that make sense and are achievable

Example question: How willing are you to get the house ready for sale?
Follow-up example: Playing back what I heard, is there anything I am missing?

Example question: What will help you stay motivated and on track?
Follow-up example: What do you need from me to take the next step?

Competency area: Action
Objective: Client articulates clear actions that they can achieve confidently

Example question: Are you in a position to make an offer today?
Follow-up example: Who are the other people you need to consult with?

Example question: What other steps need to be accomplished in order to make an offer?
Follow-up example: What further information or resources do you need to move ahead?

Competency area: Results
Objective: Client articulates how they will move forward to achieve results

Example question: What have you learned through our conversation today?
Follow-up example: Is there anything else that we need to address?

Example question: So, shall we move onto the paperwork that we need to complete?
Follow-up example: Is there anything else I can do to help keep us on track?

These are simple examples of powerful questions and follow-ups. If we look at the elevator panel again, the powerful questions frequently take us down a level, and with a great follow-up, perhaps even lower into P2. This is a key skill to be aware of and develop.

Also, be aware of the differences between open-ended and closed-ended questions. Typically, open-ended questions that start with "who, what, where, when and how" cannot be answered with a yes or a no. Closed-ended questions can be and they serve to narrow things down to a yes or no decision. For example, "do you want to buy this property?" The beauty of open-ended questions is that they serve your working partnership really well by opening up all kinds of exploratory conversational opportunities.

Powerful questions that involve visualization

Visualization is a term I use for an exciting element aimed at breathing fresh life into a traditional buyer presentation. It takes a normal needs assessment (questions such as, "How many bedrooms do you need? Bathrooms? Square footage? Age?" etcetera) and builds it into a potentially very creative and inspiring glimpse into the future. The idea is to invite your buyer to express their desires in a visual form and give you both a quick idea of the end objective. Here's how this plays out:

"I am getting a good sense of what type of property you're looking for. Can we have a bit of fun? Let's imagine you have the key in the front door lock of your ideal new home and then turn it to open the door ... can you describe for us what's inside?"

As the buyer starts exploring their mind, they might share back, "Well, there are gleaming hardwood floors, a white kitchen with granite counters and a breakfast bar, a spacious master suite with its own bathroom, second bedroom and bathroom ... lots of light."

You can help nudge thoughts along with some gently probing and prompting questions. "What else is in that picture? A fireplace? Which floor is it on and which direction does it face?"

As they unpack the vision for their ideal home, they are engaging their heart and mind in alignment which, as we discovered in our framework, can be highly inspiring. It is more sensory than: "We want two beds, two baths," and with further lines of questioning, you can really home in on that good old factor: their underlying motivation to bring it to life.

"Thanks for sharing that—sounds lovely! So, on a scale of one to ten, how important is it for us to achieve that vision for you?"

"I'd say about a ten! Time to buy; been renting long enough."

How can we do a more effective job in helping our clients decide where they want to buy?
If we refer back to the "Buyers are Liars" section earlier, we identified that geography is a real challenge in expensive

markets. The closer in to a major centre we are, the more upwardly spiralling the real estate prices can be.

Think how quickly many initial buyer conversations have the potential to become negative:

"Well, the good news is we can find you a condo like that in your price range. The bad news is that we'll be looking way out in the suburbs, based on your budget." A well-intentioned and realistic comment that describes the reality but causes immediate negativity.

If we take a similar visualization approach to "area" as we do to turning the key in the lock, are we not able to deflect away from negative emotions and instead focus in on what is really important? That could sound like something along these lines:

"Okay, you have painted a beautiful picture of what is inside your next home without us actually identifying any specific building. Now, can I encourage you to think about and describe the features you would like to see in the home's neighbourhood, without identifying that geographically either?"

"Sure. There's a coffee shop within walking distance ... major stores and a good elementary school are within say a ten- to fifteen-minute drive. There are good nature walks and it's a safe, friendly area to live. Also, road or train access to work is important so that the commute is manageable."

So far, we have asked our buyer to identify what the home and the neighbourhood look like. We have not yet drilled down into specifics.

"So, to recap, if I can find that type of property within that type of neighbourhood, would you want to see it?"

"Absolutely"

The Lower Mainland of British Columbia is a good example of this, with thousands of buyers making positive and, in the end, happy decisions to buy further out than they had first intended. It is a reality of an expensive real estate zone. By plugging in the power of visualization, we create energy, we inspire, and we challenge our buyers to think differently, and this further builds out our partnership.

In an earlier section we had talked about price reduction conversations and how to engage lifestyle impact within that realm. To me, visualization is as important in a buyer discussion.

I challenge you to add visualization to your tool chest!

Summary of core principles and self-reflection

Our learning objectives were to understand:
- **The skills that provide an exciting growth edge for you as a real estate professional**
- **How to build the bridge between *asking* to *advising***
- **The power of providing positive feedback for questions**
- **How important silence can be in creating thinking space**
- **Heading to source before solution**
- **What active listening really is and the power of great questions**
- **Exciting new visualization techniques for your clients**

There are lots of valuable skills here that provide a great opportunity to set yourself apart in the business or organization you are in. How can you use these to better engage clients in your realm?

Here are your questions:

Operational mode:
What opportunities are there for you to encourage your clients to visualize their objectives and articulate them?

Is your default to head to the source of your client's objectives, or to the solution?

How do you value your own intuition and instincts? Are they right more than they are wrong for you?

Conversational mode:
How are your abilities to sense things that surface (or don't!) in a conversation?

What do you need to focus on to be able to effectively cross the transitional bridge from *asking* to *advising*?

Do you use positive acknowledgment to handle tougher client questions?

How do you rate your listening abilities? From which perspective do you typically find yourself focusing?

How powerful are your questions? What about the quality and relevancy of follow-up questions?

What's behind the scenes for you?
How comfortable are you with silence? Is it awkward for you? What do you need to make that golden?

What action steps within your control are required to stimulate more powerful conversations and help enact meaningful change and better empowered client decisions?

Can you now build deeper, more effective working relationships with your clients?

Summary

If we link back to the beginning of our learning journey, the intention at the start of this book was to deliver to you a simple, easy-to-understand blend of competencies and a fresh perspective on the traditional real estate conversation. How have we done?

I have lost count of the number of times an agent has said to me, sometimes with head in hands or with just a slow shake of the head, how differently they would have interacted with their clients had they known about these frameworks and competencies when they started their careers. Indeed, these concepts can be great levelers for those who are newer to the business.

Many have shared with me how abundant the traditional sales methodology and training was online and how they allowed themselves to be heavily influenced by it as they started their careers. While acknowledging some value from these resources, many took away from it a need to act, *present*, handle objections and talk in a certain way, rather than just be themselves and adopt a genuine curiosity.

What have you discovered in this book? About yourself, about your past interactions, and about the potential of future ones? Are you now better equipped to have a *different* conversation and build value in a *different* way?

As you reflect on what you have gleaned from this book, doesn't coaching your clients make sense? It is the polar opposite to the *control* and *command* way of leading conversations that is part of the reason our industry has the reputation it does.

You now have a clear choice: do you head into a conversation to do most of the talking and to search for opportunities to justify your professional existence and *present* why you should be the agent of choice? Or do you refresh your approach to authentically finding out what your client needs from the conversation, co-creating and sharing an agenda as you go, and then building a strong foundation for your working partnership? You can join me in playing a key role in building new, richer value in our industry and standing out by the way you listen rather than by the amount you talk.

Epilogue

It is a wonderful thing to walk into a room and sit across from a potential or present client, totally unencumbered by pre-determined thoughts, judgements, opinions, and expectations of outcome. It is very freeing, positive, and full of possibility. A calmness pervades, and opportunities to make a difference for that person abound. It's like a blank canvas that invites creativity.

Being comfortable walking into a meeting like that can take a lot of adjustment for a service professional who is accustomed to doing most of the talking, presenting, and leading. Yet, as a starting point, it is surprising what the simplest of adjustments can do—for example, in simplest terms, when you hear yourself *tell* something, try placing a question mark at the end of sentence and ask it instead.

In coaching circles, I understand that there are many different viewpoints on what coaching is or should be. My training and adherence to the ICF framework means that coaching, to me, does not involve giving advice. However, when I contemplate introducing coaching principles into the world of business and service professional/client relationships, I put forward that it is imperative to understand and acknowledge that there is actually a wonderful, exciting co-existence between coaching and mentoring.

For example: a real estate professional is hired to provide certain professional services that are licensed under specific laws and regulations, including those that govern how clients are represented and what they can expect in terms of service and conduct. It is unrealistic to suggest that an agent can simply coach their clients, as there are requirements that must be adhered to, and professional advice, knowledge, and procedural know-how are elements that have been contracted for. I look at mentoring as the advice and know-how portion—an absolute necessity for your clients. The artful opportunity lies in how you and your client interact and partner in reaching a successful conclusion.

The key here is to understand value, and the goal is to deliver a brilliant balance between coaching and mentoring. As I said, it is not possible to merely coach a professional services client who has contracted for more than just coaching services, as there has to be an exchange of knowledge and subject-matter expertise. It is also not possible to purely *present* and *tell* without any coaching, as there are underlying motivations, needs, and concerns that have to be uncovered. If you get that balance right, the value to the recipient can be tremendous, through client-generated solutions that are arrived at through coaching and enhanced by sharing professional knowledge and expertise in a spontaneous way.

In reality, all service professionals ask some questions of their clients, as it is a basic requirement. The challenge is to turn those old conversations on their heads and truly *ask* and *engage* rather than *tell* and *present.*

The exciting vision I have is dependent upon identifying a substantial overlap in the two professions of real estate sales and coaching. That is one of the driving forces behind writing this book—not to try to turn agents into coaches, but to understand how coaching concepts fit into their real estate businesses.

Looking from another angle, what if you choose not to coach your clients? How do I answer the agent who tells me, "I've been selling real estate the same way for thirty-plus years and it has always worked using a *lead* and *present* style"?

Can you sell real estate that way? Absolutely. Will you still be able to build a successful career that way in future? Maybe. Of course, there will always be professionals in any field who have a natural, almost magnetic attraction and big, winning personalities that enable them to operate in that way, yet for most, failing to adjust from "presentation mode" to "conversation mode" runs the risk of becoming less competitive as others master deeper communication skills.

The question to ponder is: do you want to run the risk of becoming outmoded and less able to make a lasting impression with your clients as time passes, or do you want to be a standard bearer for your industry and accept coaching as the modern foundation of client communication?

The past provides clues to the future. We used to be able to sell real estate using catalogues, hand-written contracts, fax machines, and desk telephones. That was how it was done. We had all the information. What if we were still trying to operate within the structure of those times today? It would seem ridiculous.

The power of providing facts and information by harnessing ever-improving presentation technologies suggests to us that we are well served by mastering presentation and keeping on top of such advances. I absolutely agree that currency and technology adoption is essential for professional service providers; however, no matter how great your presentation skills are, everyone knows that consumers of pretty much everything have more access than ever to information, and if you fail to embrace a coaching model with your clients and continue to dominate conversation through presentation, your value level may be challenged by those who have also mastered conversational interactions.

If we know that many consumers consider real estate sales professionals to be commodities, then how curious are you to de-commoditize yourself in the eyes of those consumers?

Coaching is here to stay. If we engage a client from the standpoint of "let's imagine the possibilities," we have potential to build a wonderful alliance to collaboratively investigate a purchase or sale decision and work through the gears towards change and a positive outcome.

By exercising curiosity, you build connection.

Welcome to the wonderful world of coaching. I applaud you for taking the time to read this book and wish you all the very best as you reflect, reframe, and refine your conversations. Enjoy your reframed and spontaneous presentations, your shared agendas, and enhancing your role as a **critical thinking partner** for your clients!

Manufactured by Amazon.ca
Bolton, ON

10219141R00146